Rock Gardens
and
Alpine Plants

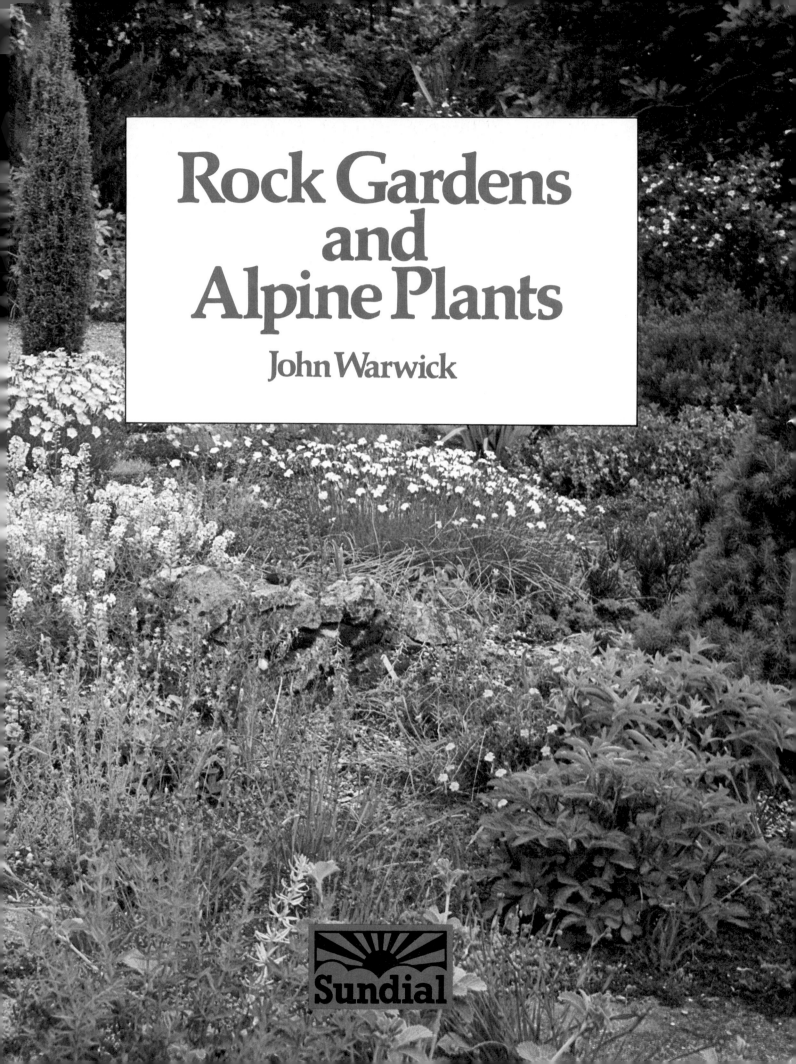

Rock Gardens
and
Alpine Plants

John Warwick

Sundial

Contents

HALF-TITLE: Soldanella alpina *in close up.*
TITLE: *A profusion of alpines in a pavement site.* CONTENTS: *Alpines and stone in the right proportions each showing off the other.*

First published in 1981
by Octopus Books Limited
59 Grosvenor Street, London W1

© 1981 Hennerwood Publications Limited

ISBN 0 906320 20 8

Printed in England
by Severn Valley Press Limited

Introduction

One of the most successful ways of filling a garden space with colour and beauty for many months of the year is to introduce alpine plants into it. The idea of combining rocks and plants to form a miniature alpine landscape has been with us for a long time, but over the last decades gardeners, both amateur and professional, have extended the definition of a rock garden, so that it now includes plantings in revamped stone sinks, the cracks between paving stones, and raised beds.

In this book you will find instructions for building both a rock garden and a scree from scratch, and for rebuilding within an existing and possibly established garden. Also, for those of you with smaller spaces, or even no garden at all, there are details on growing alpine plants in sinks, raised beds, on pavements and lawns. The designs have been chosen to last for 30 years; the plantings for 15–20 years, with minor changes.

Alpine plants are generally dwarf and the group includes those plants associated with the wild open spaces of mountains, meadows and semi-deserts, most of which have a snow covering for at least some of their winter months. They are found in most parts of the world, including the higher regions of Equatorial Africa and South America and a successful rock garden can be a true travelogue, conjuring up the natural habitats of the very different kinds of alpines it contains.

Part of the pleasure to be gained from growing alpine plants in any kind of rock garden is the wide variety of colours and shapes which the flowers, leaves and even fruits, exhibit. In fact, for small space gardening alpines offer a greater range than any other kind of plant, except maybe houseplants.

As occupational therapy gardening can have few equals and growing alpines must rate higher than most. To start with, the construction itself is exciting. Then comes the choice of plants. Next there is the thrill of

Abundant alpines on a bank: Alyssum, Arabis and Aubrieta.

planting and seeing them grow.

Whichever design you choose to follow, the idea is to grow as large a variety of plants as possible within a given area, using the method of construction best suited to your garden. I cannot stress too strongly how important it is that, regardless of the method you are adopting, the construction is well done; corrections later are most difficult and maintenance will become sheer drudgery instead of the pleasure it should be. Poor construction is not only aesthetically displeasing, it is also frustrating because it means that plants cannot grow well.

It is often thought that rock gardens must be built on a slope but, although this can increase the range of plants grown, it is not necessary. A flat site can be perfectly satisfactory for building raised beds, rock gardens, sinks, alpine lawns and pavements but the last-mentioned must have a low enough water table for the roots to reach but not cause water-logging at any time of the year.

Creating a raised bed or preparing a sink garden is an ideal way to allow everyone to see plants closely without treading all over the soil, and these kinds of gardens are especially suited to elderly or disabled people, who can grow and tend their own choice of plants at a height most comfortable to them.

Sink gardens, the smallest sites, are the most appropriate for a balcony. The flowers will be far longer lasting than those usually grown in a window box and, although the plants and flowers will be smaller, the hazards of climate will be no problem at all.

The smallest back or front garden can accommodate sinks or a pavement, or both, or even take a small raised bed.

A larger garden can take a small rock garden, one or more raised beds, sinks, a pavement, a scree, an alpine lawn, or combinations of all these. The garden may already be established, or partly so, and ready for changes, and a more ambitious scheme such as building a pond may be considered but that is outside the

range of this book. Whatever is decided, the eventual size of any construction must be in proportion to the surrounding garden. This is relatively easy in a new garden, but an established one will need more consideration, especially where trees and large shrubs may have to be removed to achieve the correct scale.

One very important requirement for alpine plant growing is the complete absence of perennial weeds. Annuals may be overcome by weeding and digging, but if perennial weeds exist at all they will spread their roots under stones and in crevices from which they can never be removed, except by moving the stones themselves. So, if a site harbours any perennial grasses, *Oxalis* (those found growing in the garden, as opposed to those good species introduced), bindweed, ground elder, or couch, it must be cleared entirely before any improvement is contemplated. Should any perennial weeds appear either in the pots of alpines when planting them out or as seeds arriving from nearby sites, they must be removed immediately or the ground will revert to its original state within a year.

Very few gardens offer ideal conditions for every type of plant and this will have a limiting effect on the choice of plants but a more important factor is the size of the garden and, as a result, the amount of light it offers. Overhanging and nearby trees present an added limitation because of drip and leaf-fall. Many alpines like sunny, well-drained situations and in damp conditions will succumb to a fungal infection known as 'damping off'. Shade cast by fences and buildings will not be a disadvantage, provided that there is no dripping water from leaking gutters.

In the table at the end of Chapter Four I have tried to represent the variety of plants you can choose from and have selected mostly tried and tested species and varieties, including some of the more difficult ones as a challenge. I have kept the larger plants to a minimum, for the space they take up generally prohibits experimentation with many varieties.

Chapter one

Alpines

The weather and soil conditions on mountains are often so extreme that the plants which grow there suffer certain distortions and need to evolve new growing methods in order to survive. On the higher plateaux, plants are dwarfed by wind and cold, and reduced to flattened or hummocked specimens. They may be found growing in between clefts of rock, or on rough ground of broken stone or small patches of soil. It is essential that the roots can grow down to a good depth, to provide support against the extremes of heat or cold, rain and wind.

Coming down the mountainside to lower levels we find several kinds of taller and bushier plants, many of them herbaceous. In order to survive the harsh winters, growth of the roots and buds is arrested until the warmer weather encourages them to start growing again. Interspersed here and there will be dwarf shrubs and trees, not artificially created like the Japanese 'bonsai' plants but species dwarfed by the elements.

Many dwarf plants at all levels survive both the cold of the winter and the dry heat of summer by growing food storage organs, mainly bulbs, often deep underground. They supply the above-ground parts, the flowers and leaves, with food until the rains or melted snows moisten the ground after long periods of drought.

Swampy ground occurs at various altitudes but more usually at lower levels. Bog plants grow here. Meadows, too, are found at various

Alpines in the wild, growing in a meadow, with a wealth of colour fit for your garden.

heights, many receiving rain throughout the year; some with a dry period. Herbaceous perennials and bulbs will grow in these conditions.

The climate in Britain is rarely anything like the natural climates of these plants, yet we can simulate them to some extent, and the more we do, the more successful will be the results. The task is to try to combine as many of these characteristics as possible within your garden and to find what grows best. The amount of light available to true alpines is often difficult to reproduce, as there are no houses, large trees and fences on mountains! However, rock shading and baking does occur. Also short plants growing in meadows are shaded and therefore are cooler at the base but receive light and warmth from the sun on the flowers and upper growths. So, if all these conditions are present in your garden anything is possible. However, if, like the majority of people, you have only some of these, your selection of plants will be limited.

From the point of view of overall construction of a rock garden, the shape and appearance of the individual plants are more important than their flowers. The plants will still be seen out of season, so those selected must give form in sufficient numbers to be of interest throughout the year. The flowers, when they do come, will be a bonus. The main categories to choose from are the short herbaceous plants and bulbs, the cushion and trailing plants, and dwarf trees, shrubs and conifers.

The mainstay of alpine plants are the mat, hummock and rosette-forming species, all of which require good drainage. They can be used in

spring, but it is in fact possible to achieve colour and interest throughout the year.

Plants ordered by post and received during very wet weather, should be placed under glass or a clear polythene cover stretched over a wooden frame until conditions are drier. If they arrive during frosty weather, again place under a cover and use leaves, straw or newspaper as a temporary plunging material. Never place the plants in a dark corner – dry and frost-proof though it may be, the lack of light will cause a rapid deterioration in the condition of the plants. They are better off outside under a cover which will let light through.

Some of the plants listed may be obtained from garden centres and general nurseries and the majority will be easily available from nurseries specializing in alpines and rock garden plants. A few will be harder to obtain. They can also, of course, be grown from seed, as explained in Chapter Three.

Which Plants and How Many?
When making a selection of plants for any kind of rock garden, it is best to draw up a plan on paper first. Decide how many and which kind of dwarf trees and shrubs to plant; always singly, never in groups. Aim for an underestimate, as one or two may be added later; an overestimate will mean either scrapping a few, or replanting elsewhere in the garden. Next choose the mat-forming, cushion and trailing plants, followed by the herbaceous varieties and, last of all, the bulbs. It is best to plant mat or cushion and herbaceous plants singly or in groups of three or five of the same kind, depending on the sizes of plants and of the site. Odd numbers give an informal effect. With bulbs you are dealing with greater numbers but remember that some species produce large foliage in relation to the size of the flowers. Planting them in groups of five, in multiples of ten, fifteen, and so on, is a useful system. Bulbs are the main features in an alpine lawn. A minimum of 10 is needed to give suf-

rock gardens, screes, raised beds and pavements, as long as there is a good depth of well-drained soil. They will generally require a reasonably light situation, free from the cover of trees and shrubs and the resulting falling leaves. The hummock type is often excellent for sink gardens, provided the sinks are deep enough. The leaves of most species are small, which means that overcrowding by taller and leafier specimens must be avoided, otherwise the growth above ground will rot, due to the lack of light and the fact that moisture is trapped in during cold spells.

Planning and Buying
The advantage of alpines and rock garden plants is the ease of buying. With few exceptions, they are grown in containers and may be planted at any time of the year, as and when they are seen on visiting a nursery. It is a mistake to do too much impulse buying, although some is inevitable, and plans will then have to be changed accordingly. Try to see plants at different times of the year, not just in the spring when the greatest number will be in flower. There is a myth that alpines and rock gardens are only worth seeing in the

Gentiana acaulis flowering in spring on limestone soil in full sun.

ficient effect and considerably more can be planted. For the larger lawns one or a few dwarf conifers can be grown to add effect during the dormant period of bulbs. The conifers can be transplanted to the lawn when they outgrow a rock garden.

There are no hard and fast rules for numbers of plants; this depends on your own personal tastes and interests at the time. Tastes will change and future replanting and gap-filling will allow for some of these changes.

However, when planning which plants should go where, remember that where alpines have been planted between stones during construction, it is rarely possible to replant after construction is completed.

For crevices on a larger site, you could plan to plant one or two dwarf shrubs but remember that they will spread forwards as well as upwards and sideways across the stone. When calculating how many crevice plants to buy, take into account that the area near the top should be left bare to allow for trailing plants in the soil above to cascade over the stones.

In a sink garden, always grow one example of each sort of plant, except for bulbs. You can plant up to five bulbs to maintain scale and variety but use only the smallest to keep their leaves from overcrowding.

Alpine herbaceous perennials grow in the whole spectrum of situations, from permanently moist to relatively dry; from deep shade to full sun. However, if they are bought when dormant, or only showing resting buds you must allow for subsequent growth. Do not put comparatively large growers close to cushion plants. The tall ones, over 40 cm (15 in), mentioned throughout the text, are suitable for the lowest level of planting in moist situations on the larger sites, where they give balance and focal points in spring and summer. This is the situation in which they are found in the wild state. No herbaceous plants are recommended for pavements as the resting buds are liable to be accidentally trodden on in winter.

Bulbs and corms add a fascinating mixture to any site. Their moisture requirements are variable but most require plenty of light, at least in the spring. In many cases, especially in limited space, you can add extra colour by planting them under dwarf shrubs which lack winter foliage. All bulbs and corms have a dormant period but unlike herbaceous plants they do not have resting buds to indicate their positions, so they should be marked on to the plan. This can save the embarrassment of digging them up when planting in an apparently empty space!

Having made careful choices and planned the layout of your site, you must now plant the alpines in their new home. Many people rate planting-out as the second most exciting part of gardening – following close behind propagation. You must exercise great care to ensure that the right plants are put in the positions you envisaged for them and they must be placed in the ground just as they were when you received them or as they are in your own propagation container. Resist the temptation to put the plants just a little deeper. Although this may be worthwhile with some plants, alpines resent this kind of treatment and will quite likely rot away.

Chapter two

Stone & Soil

Stone

The rock gardener is faced with a wide choice of stones, but they all fall into two basic types: sandstones and limestones. Sandstones were formed over millions of years as successive deposits of silt hardened to form layers, or strata, of stone. When cut, sandstone splits vertically, along 'vents', a process which can also occur naturally as a result of upward pressure; and horizontally, along the lines of the strata. They are thus easily cut into block shapes of various sizes. These blocks may be used for making raised beds as they can be laid, layer after layer, like the dry stone walls surrounding farms in some stoney areas.

Slates are sandstones which developed on the earth's surface but were eventually buried many thousands of feet below it forming, under the terrific pressures, very thin wafer-like structures. When placed on their edges slates are very brittle but if laid horizontally they create exceptionally strong structures.

Limestones may be formed in a similar way to sandstones but more usually they derive from the crushed bodies of vast numbers of crustacean insects and vertebrate animals which, under pressure for millions of years, form into irregular layers of stone. With careful selection these asymmetrical stones can be made to fit together like a jigsaw puzzle, or used to create a series of layers at different levels, with scattered pockets of soil between. They are admirable for use in screes either singly or in twos or threes.

A lewisia hybrid in tufa rock, with plant and stone ideally suited.

A form of limestone called tufa stone deserves a mention here. It is a light porous stone, ideal for limited spaces as it enables you to grow many small plants, both in the stones and the soil beneath them. The surface is quite soft and can be punctured with holes, cut out with a hammer and chisel or a drill. The holes, which should not be too wide, are ideal for supporting the young seedlings or rooted cuttings of any alpines requiring good drainage. A plug of mortar (five parts of sand to one part of cement) pressed on two-thirds of the soil surface in the holes after planting, will ensure that the plants and the soil will stay put and be less likely to dry out. You can use an old-fashioned potato peeler for sliding the seedling into the hole and a ball-point pen for ramming the soil in after it. A potato peeler is also useful for weeding in the tufa blocks.

Limestones

Westmorland	Cheddar
Tufa	Purbeck
Cotswold	Mendip
Dorset	

Sandstones and Slates

Sussex	Dean
Ham	Devon
Millstone Grit	Cornish Slate
Pennant	Welsh Slate
Somerset	York

Do not use any stone formed volcanically in this country, that is marble or Aberdeen granite, as these have the wrong character for rock garden or wall building.

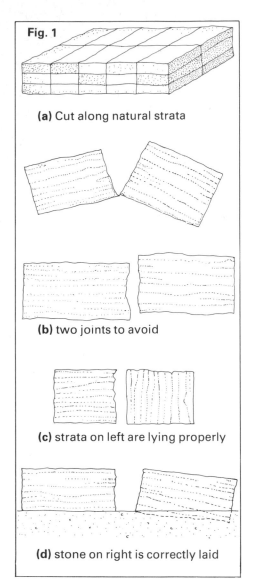

Fig. 1

(a) Cut along natural strata

(b) two joints to avoid

(c) strata on left are lying properly

(d) stone on right is correctly laid

Acid or Lime?

Sandstones, which are acidic, can support every type of plant, including lime-lovers. Similarly, acid-loving plants can be grown on many kinds of limestone but not those which release free lime into the soil, as it will inhibit their growth.

An excess of lime in the soil will cause the leaves of acid-loving plants to turn yellow – a condition known as 'chlorosis'. This is easily remedied by watering the soil around the bases of the affected plants with a solution made from sequestrene granules dissolved in water. In general, however, it is far better and easier to grow plants in their natural soil-types.

It is relevant here to examine what the words 'acidic' and 'limy' mean in practical terms to a rock gardener. A standard scale, known as the pH scale, is used to measure the relative acidity of many substances – including soil. It ranges between 0–14: 1–6 indicates acidity; 6.5–7.5 is neutral; 7.5–14 indicates alkalinity or, in the case of a soil sample, liminess. Simple soil-testing kits can be bought in a gardening shop and by following the maker's instructions, you can discover the type of soil in your garden, and stock it accordingly. As a double check, look at the plants growing around you – for instance, if Rhododendrons, Azaleas or heathers are thriving the soil is acidic. Though not a totally reliable test, because varia-tions can occur over very short distances, it will give a rough idea.

Types of Soil

There are many factors determining the most suitable type of soil for a rock garden. Where the garden is started from scratch you should choose the soil mix best suited to the needs of the plants you want to grow. Building raised beds and sink gardens are simple ways of achieving this. If the site already exists it may well be necessary to introduce a soil mixture nearer to the requirements of the plants desired. Lawns, pavements and rock gardens built on level ground are amenable to such changes but if the site is on a slope, it will be difficult to prevent the erosion of one type of soil into another.

If an acid soil is being introduced into a flat limestone garden, gently mound the existing soil upwards towards the centre of the site. Use a 1000 gauge black plastic liner to cover an area slightly larger than the proposed extent of the site including the mound. Then lay the stone on top of the plastic in the normal way. This will prevent stagnation and drainage problems, as well as stopping lime reaching the introduced acid soil. If a lime soil is being built over an already acid garden, there is no need for mounding or for a liner because lime will not do much harm to acid soil.

The soil mixtures already men-

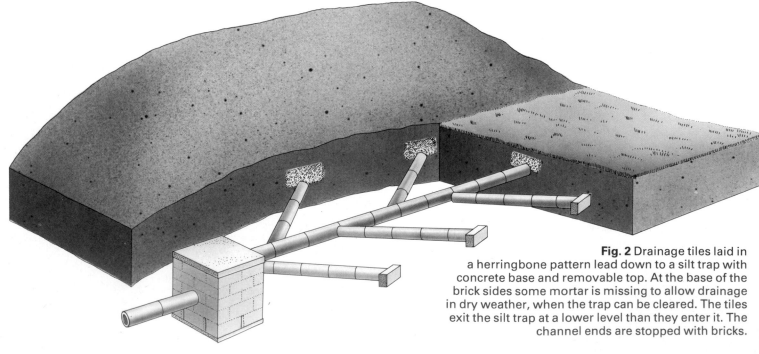

Fig. 2 Drainage tiles laid in a herringbone pattern lead down to a silt trap with concrete base and removable top. At the base of the brick sides some mortar is missing to allow drainage in dry weather, when the trap can be cleared. The tiles exit the silt trap at a lower level than they enter it. The channel ends are stopped with bricks.

tioned contain three main ingredients: humus, grit or shingle, and loam. Their proportions mainly depend on the amount of light received in the garden and its local climate. In a shady spot the mixture should contain up to 50% humus combined with equal parts of grit or shingle, and loam. In a more sunny and open setting reduce the humus content by about 25% and mix it with equal amounts of the other ingredients.

The proportions must also be varied according to the windiness of the site: with higher rainfall and less wind on a site, more shingle or grit will be needed to give better drainage, and vice versa.

Apply these mixtures to the top 30–38 cm (12–15 in) of soil layer of any ground. Again, the depth varies according to the natural underlying soils; the better the drainage, the shallower the top layer can be, but it must never be less than 15 cm (6 in).

A note here about the term 'humus'. It can be considered to be peat and leafmould, with more of the latter in preference. The quality of loams is very variable, so an explanation of good loam may also help. An ideal loam is the layer of soil immediately below meadow grass; the grass roots give it a fibrous texture and being neither sand nor clay it can be easily crumbled in the hands. Because it contains perennial weed seeds it must always be sterilized before use.

Grits and shingles are coarser than sands and vary in texture and size, the grains ranging from 2 to 30 mm ($\frac{1}{12}$ to $1\frac{1}{4}$ in) in diameter. Their presence in a soil mixture enables effective drainage: the coarser the grains, the better the drainage. If the grains are large enough and in sufficient quantity they will hold some moisture underneath, be able to maintain many plants and there will be no danger of overwatering.

Drainage

There should be no need to fit drainage tiles to most raised sites for alpines, unless the soil is heavy clay or the water table is high. The water table is the level to which water rises in the ground under normal conditions. If this is just below the surface of the soil, then drains are essential; if above, then you should take up

water gardening not alpine plant growing! To check for a high water level in the soil, dig a hole at the lowest point in the garden. Any water appearing in that hole will indicate the level of water.

Where the water table is just below the ground, flooding can obviously occur, so choose the highest ground possible and fit 30 cm by 10 cm (12 in by 4 in) tiles to run the water off. Lay these just above the normal water table level by hollowing out the soil to fit the tiles and no more; then put a layer of gravel on top of the tiles. Provided there is a slope or at least a fall of 1 in 200 for the drains and somewhere for the water to drain to, the whole garden can be drained without any problems, see figure 2.

The same principle applies for tile draining on heavy clay soils but the depth to which the tiles can be laid is greater. Note that if they are buried deeper than 60 cm (2 ft) at any point they will be ineffective. It is important not to lay more than 10 cm (4 in) of gravel over the tiles or this will be disturbed by cultivations.

A similar procedure is carried out when building drains under a lawn but in this case the gravel should be covered by fine nylon mesh to prevent soil being washed down to the gravel and thence to the tiles. There is no need to drain more than 22 cm (9 in) below the grass level.

The details for drainage are intended for the garden as a whole and cover all sites and constructions considered in this book, except rock gardens, which are dealt with separately in Chapter Four.

Watering

Methods of watering are best kept as simple as possible, with a sprinkler, preferably with a spike in the base, on the end of a hosepipe, for example. Much more important, however, are the questions of when and how often to apply the water. The table at the end of Chapter Four lists the moisture requirements of each plant. All categories can be watered by the same sprinkler by watering to suit the middle range plants when one or two are just beginning to show signs of flagging. Alternatively, water just those plants requiring water by hand.

In their first season in the garden, plants will require more watering than successive seasons, so that watering by hand is often best. Use a sprinkler for the successive seasons but less often, in order to encourage the roots to grow downwards rather than sideways. When plants are in need of water those with soft foliage remain turgid or firm in the leaves but when too dry, they droop or flag.

Lewisia cotyledon, *a beautiful rosette plant for well-drained conditions.*

Chapter three

Propagation

Seeds

Probably the most exciting part of gardening is producing new plants and growing alpines is no exception. Many may be reproduced by very simple means; the easiest and best method is to grow them from seed. Unfortunately few firms sell alpine seeds but those who do are well worth contacting. Alternatively you could join the Alpine Garden Society or the Scottish Rock Garden Club, both of whom issue large annual seed lists to their members and will give excellent advice.

Alpine seeds come in a variety of shapes and sizes, each requiring a different method of sowing. Large seeds like *Sorbus* are sown individually, whereas very fine dustlike seeds such as *Haberleas* can be mixed with dry sand to make sowing more even and feathery seeds like those of the *Pulsatillas* are teased out and flattened on the surface of the sowing medium. Seeds of an average and manageable size can be sown straight from the packet or by dropping them from a folded sheaf of paper.

Seeds may be sown in a variety of containers but porous clay pots are probably the most satisfactory. Place a crock over the drainage hole, if it is large enough to lose soil through, and fill the container with a soil mixture to within 2.5 cm (1 in) of the rim (when firmed down) for large and feathery seeds, slightly higher for small ones. Sow the seeds and cover with 5 mm (¼ in) of pea gravel or shingle: a single layer for the finer seeds, slightly more to hold down

The pulsatilla *on the left has produced plentiful seedheads. The feathery seeds are teased out before sowing.*

the larger and feathery seeds. The sown seeds must lie thinly, otherwise when they have germinated their roots will entangle, making separation difficult, and causing damage which may destroy the plants.

Use a gritty soil mix; equal amounts of John Innes seed compost and grit or fine shingle, which must be acidic for all acid-loving plants.

No heating is required to germinate alpine seeds and, apart from during wet weather, no frame cover either, but plunging the pots in coarse sand or grit will reduce the need for watering. The shingle layer over the seeds prevents heavy rain dislodging the seeds from the pots.

Place the containers in a cool place out of direct sunlight, in an open frame until germinated. Then cover the pots, when wet, with either a glass or a plastic cover at an angle to reduce drips from condensation, see figure 3. The frame should face north but if this is not possible, shade it with nylon shading material until the seeds have germinated. The shade lovers can remain in the frame until large enough to handle whilst you should move the remainder into more light on germination. When the first leaf or pair of leaves, the cotyledons, appear you may begin transplanting or 'pricking out'. It is easier to pot individually into 60 to 75 mm (2.5 to 3 in) pots, but where space is limited seed trays or similar containers can be used. When roots begin to fill the containers, plant the seedlings into their permanent positions. An ideal repotting mixture for seedlings contains 50% John Innes No. 1 potting compost, with 20% extra peat, and 30% extra grit.

Division

Propagation by division is a simple method and it produces instant results which can be planted straight-away. Herbaceous plants can be divided between autumn and spring. Begin by cutting down most of the stems and leaves to within about 2.5 cm (1 in) of the soil surface. Insert two hand or border forks, back to back, down into the outer part of a lifted plant and push the forks apart. Do this as often as necessary until you have the number of plants you require. Always avoid the central crown area of any herbaceous plant, for it is woody and hard, whereas the outsides are young and fresh, and small plantlets will grow more satisfactorily than large clumps.

Cuttings

Propagation by means of cuttings is particularly appropriate for hybrids, or 'cultivars' (cultivated varieties) as they are known. These are plants which if grown from seed do not exactly reproduce the parent colour, flower or shape. Hybrids of variegated plants revert to their uniformly green form.

Cuttings should be taken from good healthy plants at times when rooting has its greatest chance of success. Wherever possible avoid taking cuttings when the plants are in full flower, because at this time most of the plant's energy is going into making the flowers and not the wood. As a general guide take cuttings shortly after flowering just as the new growth is becoming firm. Most alpines flower early and cuttings can be taken in June or July. With those plants that flower later, take cuttings of soft growth in the spring and early summer. Conifers and *Aubrietas* are exceptions; they should be taken in the autumn: September or October.

These guidelines apply to cuttings taken from the tops and sides of soft wooded plants. In the case of dwarf conifers, the cuttings must be taken from the side growths only, otherwise the resulting plants will tend to be larger, or, if the cuttings come from the bottom growths, smaller than the original.

It is always better to take small cuttings; larger ones take longer to root and are ultimately slower to

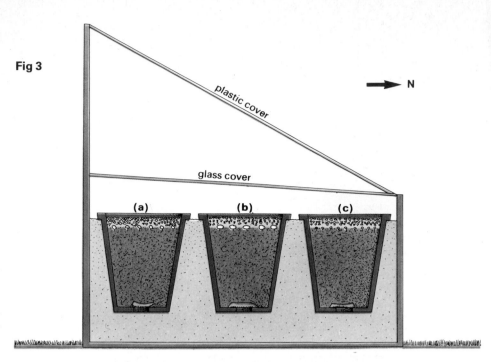

Fig 3

plastic cover

glass cover

(a)　(b)　(c)

N →

grow. Approximately 10 to 30 mm (½ in to 1¼ in) is long enough for most, although larger plants will need longer pieces. The two most common methods of taking cuttings are by nodal cuts for soft growth and heel cuts for harder, wooded stems. To take a nodal cutting, slice straight across the stem below a leaf or pair of leaves, and remove the lower leaves with a sharp knife (see figure 5 (a)). Take a heel cutting by tearing a young growth from a strong stem with a sharp downward pull; neatly trim the resulting 'heel' and remove the lower leaves (see figure 5 (b)).

Dryas octopetala *has creamy white flowers followed by these seed. heads.*

Cuttings can be planted out into almost any kind of container, but it is easier to re-pot the rooted plant if it is tipped out of a plant pot. Insert all cuttings almost up to the leaves in a mixture of equal parts of coarse sand (not soft builders' sand) and peat. Moistening the sand will make it easier to insert the woody cuttings, while an old ball point pen is ideal for planting softer ones. Keep the cuttings in a warm place if possible, but away from direct sunlight. As with

Fig. 3 Sowing **(a)** seeds of average size **(b)** large and feathery seeds **(c)** fine seeds. The frame should face north, if not shade it with nylon shading until germination. All are covered with a layer of shingle or pea gravel. The pots, plunged in coarse sand, are, when seeds have germinated, covered with glass lights at a shallow angle or plastic lights at an angle of 30° or more to reduce drips from condensation.

Fig. 4 Division: cut down stems and leaves to within 2.5 cm of the soil surface. Push two small forks, back to back, into the crown of the plant and force the forks apart.

Fig. 5 Cuttings **(a)** nodal: make a straight cut below a pair of leaves **(b)** heel: strip the cutting from wood of the previous year **(c)** root: cut tops horizontally and bases diagonally.

Fig. 6 Layering: use a peg to hold down the branch. Cover stem with about 20 mm of soil.

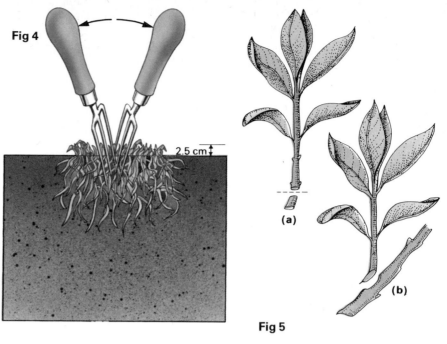

Fig 4

2.5 cm

Fig 5

Fig 6

seeds, the containers can be plunged into coarse sand or grit, to maintain an even temperature and reduce the need for watering but unlike germinating seeds, it is better to keep cuttings under glass or a plastic cover to retain warmth and some humidity until they are rooted. It is a good idea to add a proprietary copper solution when you water the plants to help prevent 'damping off'.

Watch the cuttings daily. Remove any blackened or damped-off cuttings or yellowing leaves immediately. Pot the cuttings individually when they are rooted. To test for rooting pull gently on the cuttings; if they remain firm they are ready for potting. Pot into 60 to 75 mm (2½ to 3 in) containers and leave under cover for about 10 days, then remove the cover and let them grow until they are ready to plant out. Use the same soil mixture as for repotting seedlings.

Root Cuttings
Plants which produce thick fleshy roots see page 75 can be propagated by making root cuttings. Dig out one or two roots from the soil in January to February and cut them into a series of pieces about 20 mm (¾ in) long. To ensure that you insert these cuttings the right way up, make a straight cut at the top and slice the bottom at an

angle. Bury the entire cutting under the sand and keep the containers almost dry until growth appears on the surface.

Layering
Layering is a simple method of reproduction, ideally suited to those plants such as Rhododendrons which produce woody stems at fairly low levels. Choose one or more branches whose growth is reasonably flexible and scratch out the soil immediately below. Replace the original soil with sand, if the plant requires well-drained conditions, or sand and leaf

mould for woodland types, like Rhododendrons.

Pin the branch down into its new position with a peg of hazel wood or a piece of wire, and cover the stem with about 20 mm (¾ in) of soil. Gently bend the branch almost vertical, just past the peg and tie it to a bamboo cane, in that position. If the peg begins to rise, weight it down with a stone (see figure 6).

If layering is done in the spring, the new plant should have rooted by the following spring and can be cut from the parent plant and transplanted, in the autumn.

A rock garden on a sloping site showing plenty of colour.

Chapter four

Rock Gardens

Site

The first decision to make when building a rock garden is where to site it. This will also determine the construction of the garden and what plants it contains. The ideal site will have no trees or shrubs nearby to cast shade and cause drips, or to provide fatal leaf cover to plants which naturally grow in the open.

Having chosen the site, draw a plan of the garden as it exists. A rough sketch is perfectly adequate, as long as it shows all the main features – the buildings, fences, walls, borders, trees and large shrubs. Make two copies of the plan; onto one shade in the area receiving the estimated maximum amount of sunshine (if any) in midwinter; then do the same for midsummer on the other. In a site with little sunshine in midwinter, you can grow those plants in the tolerant range, shown on the table at the end of the chapter as sun/shade. A garden which is really sunny in winter and summer can accommodate the greatest range of plants, provided some shade is created within the rock garden. Most gardens fall in between these extremes, having good summer sunshine but mainly poor winters, with only small areas getting the maximum sunshine.

Before construction can begin it is essential to consider two points about the site: perennial weeds and drainage.

Weeds

As mentioned in the introductory chapter, perennial weeds are those which remain permanently in the ground. They fall into three major categories: those with small bulbs (bulbils), such as *Oxalis* and *Allium*: plants which spread by means of runners or stolons, such as couch, bindweed, clover, creeping buttercup, ground elder, speedwell and sorrel; and plants with thickened root-stocks, such as dandelion, dock and Welsh poppy, see figure 8. It is often difficult to remove these weeds completely in one attempt, either by hand or using weedkillers, especially when they grow amongst the roots of garden plants.

Very often rock gardens are built on sites previously planted with grass. If the grasses were fine, without runners and stolons preparation of the site simply involves clearing an area about 1 metre (3 feet) greater than that required for the rock garden. However, this is often far from the case, and usually weeds of all sorts, including running grasses, abound, adding a risk that they will all creep into the rock garden.

If you wish to keep a lawn around the site, there are two possible ways of dealing with running weeds. The lawn can be completely renewed by removing all grass, applying a total weedkiller, and leaving the site fallow for three months during the growing season before beginning construction and sowing. Alternatively, most of the weeds (except grasses) can be destroyed by applying a lawn weedkiller. After a minimum of six months the site can be resown with fine grasses, with a slight risk that some weedy grasses will creep in.

If you find perennial weeds in potted or open-ground plants bought from a nursery you should remove

21

A well-established rock garden, with a gravel border to keep weeds at bay.

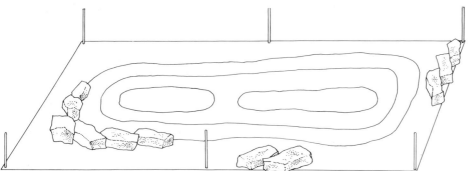

Fig. 7 Laying out the site **(a)** using rope to mark out each layer of the rock garden **(b)** cross-section of a garden built with four layers.

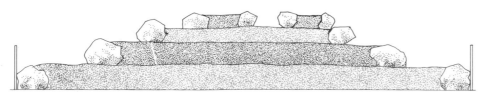

them entirely before planting, or re-port it to the nursery concerned on returning the plants. Nurseries steril-ize the soil, which is effective against most weeds but clovers remain un-affected, and they should have been removed from pots before sale.

These measures do not stop all weeds; it is essential to remove them as they appear.

Drainage

In Chapter Two we looked at methods of drainage for a whole gar-den and mentioned that a rock gar-den site may need additional care. It is obvious that any construction above ground level will create natural drainage, but the water must still be able to drain down to tiles if there are any. (Where drainage is no problem ignore the following paragraph.)

Cover the potential site with a layer about 15 cm (6 in) deep of hardcore or well-broken rubble. Top this with gravel, or very stony soil to fill the spaces created by the hardcore, and tamp the whole lot well down.

If the site has a high water table, it is worth considering making a natural pool by using the existing water table. This would be hard work because the water cannot be drained during the operation, besides which the pool could not, for practical purposes, be very deep. Alternatively you could build a rock garden above the water table and grow bog plants around its base.

It is important to realise that any construction will be raised above the existing ground level and this must be taken into account on the plan. By drawing a third sketch showing only the outlines of the boundaries of possible areas for the rock garden and the low points of the garden you can work out the problems of drainage. Planning in this way saves time, money and effort and probably a lot of disappointment.

Your final plan will only be a guide to the construction, not to be adhered to exactly because you will have to make adjustments and modifications to allow for the variety of shapes and sizes of stone that you will be handling. Very few people can visualize three dimensional design, whereas they have fewer problems in two dimensions. By visiting established rock gardens you will be able to get further ideas, and notice their mistakes and good points.

Laying Out

Once the possible site has been decided on, mark it out as a rectangle slightly larger than required. Use rope or thick string to give the informal shape within the rectangle and try to imagine the third dimension, height. This will enable you to maintain a sense of proportion with the rest of the garden, if the rock garden is only one component in a larger plan.

Proportion is essentially the balance between length, depth and height, so that, when planted, the garden does not look like a mountain or a molehill. Instead, the aim is to create a replica of a very small corner of any mountain with its plants.

Any alterations to improve the growing conditions for alpines should be carried out now *before* the construction is started, not after. Make sure that you will have no difficulties getting to the site, both with construction materials now, and for future maintenance. The way to the site will need to be both clear and wide enough to receive the necessary stone and soil.

The speed of progress will vary considerably according to the accessibility of the site, the type of soil in the garden already, and the amount of help available. You will certainly need help, the amount depending on the size of stones to be handled. Teamwork is essential when dealing with the largest stones. Construction work is heavy and exhausting, and is best done in winter when conditions are cooler.

The Raw Materials

Once the planning decisions have been made it is time to order the stone, the soil, the first batch of alpine plants to grow between the stones, the tools and equipment necessary for the project, and to solicit the help of a few friends. It is advisable to order the stone well in advance of requirement, as delivery may take some time. When ordering direct from a quarry or through an agency, specify the approximate sizes required and seek their advice as to the quantity needed for your site. Ordering too many rather than too few pieces gives a much greater choice during construction. As stones vary considerably in their size/weight ratio I will refrain from giving advice here as it could be misleading.

Soil may be obtained from suppliers to the commercial growers, whose names can be found in the telephone directory. It usefully comes in bags in most cases and usually the firm will mix ingredients according to your specification. Arrange for the soil to be delivered before the stone. If the soil is covered by empty plastic bags, an old tarpaulin or similar material, the stone can be unloaded onto the soil when it arrives. It is easier to tip a small load onto soft surfaces, rather than lift it

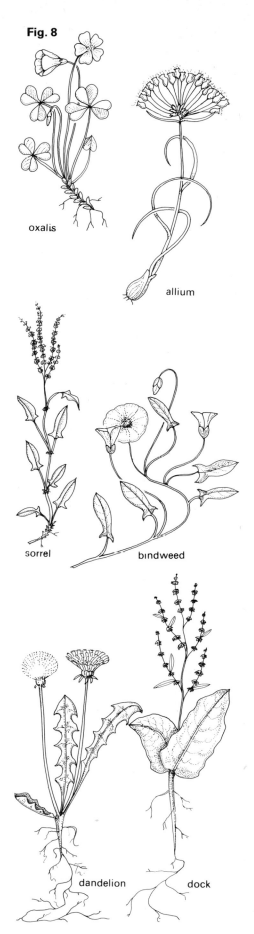

Fig. 8

oxalis

allium

sorrel

bindweed

dandelion

dock

23

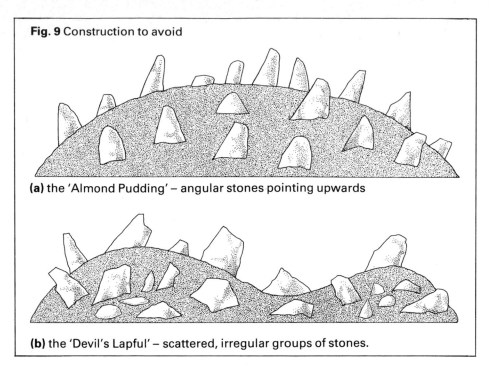

Fig. 9 Construction to avoid

(a) the 'Almond Pudding' – angular stones pointing upwards

(b) the 'Devil's Lapful' – scattered, irregular groups of stones.

down onto hard ones. For larger loads, hire a tipper lorry to dump the stone straight onto the soil (if space allows). Otherwise order smaller loads which, though more expensive will be easier to deal with. Tipping causes very little or no damage, provided the first stones fall on a soft surface.

Construction

Reginald Farrer, an early alpine enthusiast, wrote in 1909 of the various disasters which have been given the title of a rock garden. He gave them descriptive names such as 'Almond Pudding' or 'Devil's Lapful'. These collections of stone fashioned together to form a mockery of mounds are fit only for weeds or plants so tolerant of extremes of wet and dry that they defy description!

A successful rock garden should be a compromise between the wildness of a natural rocky habitat and the ordered human geometry imposed on some formal gardens; a showcase for some of the thousands of alpine plants available.

The Stones

The structure of a brick wall with its regular layers gives a very good picture of how many of our rocks, particularly sandstones, were formed. A rock garden is laid in a similar way, except that the regular-shaped bricks are replaced by the

irregular-shaped stones, giving a series of single layered terraces of informal design, laid like those found in nature, with plants on the terraces and in between the stones.

For any shape of construction try to use large stones. They are more stable than a lot of small ones and look much better. Choose stone which will suit the area and the pocket. Transport is very costly, so buy stone near home. Try to avoid rounded stones; they are difficult to bed in the ground and do not fit together well. There are exceptions though, for example, Westmorland limestone, which has no strata or line of formation and can be laid in any direction you choose, although fitting the pieces together will be rather like doing a jigsaw. It is a very heavy stone.

Sandstones, on the other hand, have definite strata, which may be hard to see at first but practice makes them easier to recognise. Always ask to be shown the direction of the strata when you buy the stone and lay it with the strata leaning gently back from horizontal, towards the centre of the site, (see figure 1). By laying a stone in the plane in which it was originally formed you can prevent frost action from splitting it and thus ruining an otherwise well-laid site. It will also make the presentation look more natural.

Some planting can be made bet-

ween the stones during construction but never try to thrust plants in between stones *after* the construction is complete as this can damage the roots. Replacement might be very difficult so you should take all possible care to select good plants and treat them accordingly. Plant on the thinnest joints, see figure 16, so that the roots grow into the soil leaving the branches on the outside.

Equipment

You will not require many tools for laying stones but some are large. The number and sizes of obvious ones – spades, forks and shovels, depend on the size of the site. Do not be tempted to use a spade for a shovel, it takes too long! Gumboots are a must; consider safety gumboots with steel toecaps – there is no V.A.T. on them! Many tools needed may be hired on a daily or weekly basis. It is a good idea to use a sack truck, which, handled by three people, will carry up to 90 kg (4 cwt) quite easily. It should preferably have pneumatic tyres rather than solid ones. Make sure there is sufficient planking to run the truck over soft ground. The most readily available are scaffold planks, which you should make into a single line for each wheel supporting up to 45 kg (2 cwt). By doubling the thickness of the planks, up to 90 kg (4 cwt) can easily be supported by the pneumatic-tyred trucks. Stone over 90 kg will require four people and single planks 7.5 × 23 cm (3 × 9 in). You will also need crowbars which can be hired and rollers.

Moving the Stones to the Site

Arrange the planks and rollers as shown in figure 10. The rollers are made of solid metal rods, 1 metre (39 in) long by 20 mm (¾ in) thick. To prevent the planks moving when you are loading or unloading, cut four wooden wedges thicker than the rollers, and place two at each end, between the upper and lower planks.

To raise a stone you require two crowbars, pointed at one end and flat at the other, and some baulks of wood to act as fulcrums and blocks, see figure 11. Railway sleepers, cut to reduce their width by half, are ideal

Ceratostigma plumbaginoides *growing below* Liriope spicata *in autumn.*

A shallow slope of rock garden in sandstone bordered on one side by grass and on the other by a gravel path.

for this purpose. The size of the crowbar depends on the size of the stone being moved: 35 mm (1.5 in) by 1.5 metre (5 ft) long works well on loads of up to 90 kg (4 cwt); over that weight use heavier crowbars (about 9 kg (40 lbs)).

To raise the stone onto a sack truck, see figure 12. Use the same technique to lift heavy stones to higher levels on the rock garden, and also onto planks and rollers. The roll-

ing movement involved in this operation makes it ideal for moving stones short distances without a sack truck but I would suggest that on soft ground planks are used to stop the surrounding site becoming a quagmire and also to prevent the stone being accidentally buried.

Reverse the process for unloading, or turn the stone end-over-end over the handles of the truck as they rest on the ground, or on the first layer of stone laid, to give an immediate gain in height.

Another method of moving stone is by using paired rope slings. This

system requires four people to work it. The slings are made of nylon rope 1.5 cm (½ in) thick, each one approximately 2 metres (6ft) long, spliced to themselves to form a ring. The slings can be used in two ways. Firstly, to lift stone weighing up to 65 kg (3 cwt) by cradling it in the rings doubled up, two people lift the stone, while another two place timber under it, in turn, until lifted to the required height. You still need one crowbar to get the slings under in the first place but this method saves time.

Secondly, the slings can be used to give a better grip when pulling stones along on rollers, see figure 13. Once the stone is lifted onto the planks, gently pull the planks along, lining up the rollers to enable the planks to be pulled round corners and carrying the rear planks and rollers to the front each time. Be careful not to topple the stone; use the crowbars to steady it, and to turn the top planks.

Laying the Stones on the Site

When the stone is on the site ready for laying, try to disturb the ground as little as possible and do not hurry the operation at any stage; accidents can happen. Place the stones in their final position, which is explained in detail later in the chapter, using the same technique as before. To move a stone forward, see figure 14 (a) and (b). Repeat the move making new holes for the crowbar so as not to disturb the ground too much.

As each layer of stone is laid fill in the soil behind it by ramming in a barrowload, until the level is just below the top of the stone laid. This will hide the bases of the next layer of stones, without having to dig very much, if any, soil out.

When a layer is completed, raise the soil level by 30 mm (1 in) for every 30 cm (1 ft) in length from one level to the next, so that the resulting hump allows for sinkage which, despite all the ramming, will occur. The soil should cover the rear of all stones, so that none are exposed to show their size. This will give the impression of the stone running back into the ground as it does in nature. As each stone is laid stand at different points in the garden to see the effect. It is surprising how it can look well from one point and not from another.

The Surrounds

Mowing the grass and maintenance of the ground around many rock gardens will be a problem, unless there are paving slabs, or stone paths between the rock garden and the lawn. Grass has a habit of creeping up and round but not through stone. The material for this purpose need not be the same as for the construction but it must be level and look reasonably similar and informal. The slabs should not be rectangular; but should be at least 30 cm (1 ft) wide. If the depth is shallower than 8 cm (3 in)

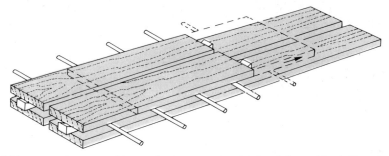

Fig. 10 Arrangement of planks and rollers for moving stone. To move planks, remove wedges, add new roller to right of planks and roll top planks on to it.

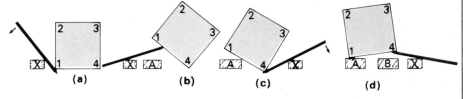

Fig. 11 Two crowbars used to push stone on to planks: **(a)** use block X as rest for crowbar **(b)** slip plank A underneath **(c)** move block X to other side **(d)** slip plank B underneath. The second crowbar not shown steadies the stone as in Fig. 12.

Fig. 12 Two crowbars and a wooden block used to lever a stone up and on to a sack truck.

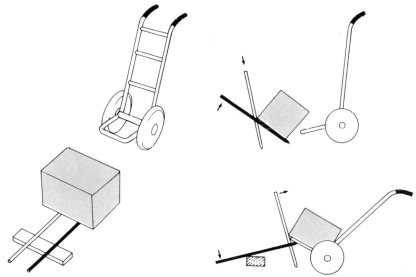

Fig. 13 A rope sling used to help pull a stone along.

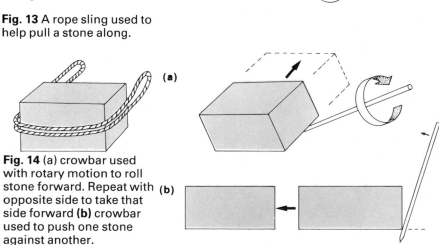

Fig. 14 (a) crowbar used with rotary motion to roll stone forward. Repeat with opposite side to take that side forward **(b)** crowbar used to push one stone against another.

they can be laid on a bed of concrete to prevent movement but the concrete should not show. To do this, roughly pattern out the stones for the site, then set them aside in order. Lay a bed of concrete 10 cm (4 in) thick. Press each stone into the mix. Before the cement sets press a layer of rubble and stone chips left over from the rock garden construction between the stones so that they lie below the surface. Laying stones on cement will inhibit the growth of weeds of any size; smaller weeds and grasses can be prevented from growing at all by applying a pre-emergence weedkiller early each year. Take care not to get any weedkiller on the lawn or rock garden. The level of the completed paving surround must be below the surrounding grass to enable the mowing machine to run over the slabs and not into them.

Keep the surrounding grass from creeping towards the rock garden by regularly trimming it with edging shears. Using a halfmoon-shaped tool each winter will make the edging easier to maintain during the growing season.

If there is a border of bare soil 8 cm (3 in) wide, between the paving and the grass, this will help to keep down the · risk of perennial weeds (see figure 15). Maintenance then means keeping that border free of weeds.

Stones, water and plants suited to well-drained and boggy conditions for a greater range of interest.

Flat Sites

When building a rock garden on a flat site, use the largest stones possible and, for practical reasons, use the tallest stones for the bottom layer. Take one of the pieces with the largest top surface and lean it backwards towards the centre of the site. Sink it just below soil level but do not bury it unnecessarily. Remove only the essential amount of soil first; it is better to remove too little at first than too much and then have to replace it with soft yielding soil which may weaken the stability of the stone being laid. When the stone is in position ram it well in before introducing the next stone.

The first stone to be laid is the keystone, from which all the others will radiate on both sides. Each stone must join exactly on to the end or face of the next one, otherwise soil will spill from the upper to lower level and the structure will be ruined. This part of construction takes a lot of time but is well worth the effort.

If the stones are wedge-shaped they can be laid with the thin end behind the last stone laid or in front, thus leaving the thicker part of the stone to fit into the rock garden and so thickening the depth, see figure 16. Minor obstructions to the line of the stones can be chipped off with a cold chisel and club hammer, or another stone chosen. The tops of all stones must be level to within 2.5 cm (1 in) of one another. If the top is not level, then when the two ends join to complete the circuit, they will not

match up on the top level and soil will spill from the upper level, exposing the back as well as the front of the stone. Check this as your work progresses around the keystone by using a spirit level (see figure 16).

You can build any shape but angular constructions look more impressive than round ones. Lay each stone with its strata almost parallel to the ground, slightly sloping backwards.

When the first layer is completed, the second and subsequent layers may be added. The base of each layer must begin below the top of the last level, see figure 18. The total number of layers will depend on the size of the project and be determined by the proportion.

Try as far as possible to arrange the greater number of surfaces facing south, east and west, for the greatest amount of sunshine and the smallest area facing the north.

Paths

Larger sites will need paths between the different sections of the rock garden. To decide whether your garden needs a path consider how easy it will be to carry out maintenance work and also whether the plants can be clearly seen from normal ground level, bearing in mind that alpine plants are generally smaller than others in a garden.

A path should be wide enough to allow two people to pass one another – since your handiwork is bound to be shown to others. Gently curved paths are more effective than angular

Fig. 15 Section through rock garden site showing outer border of turf with gap left to allow weeding. Wooden blocks hold in cement base. Paving stones laid right up to base of rock garden are set into cement and small stone chips are pressed between the stones, below the surface.

or sharp-cornered ones.

If the water table in your garden is high, build simple paths at ground level but where it is low i.e. 30 cm (1 ft) or more below the lowest point on the path, you may use a system of 'cut-and-fill' paths as described below, provided that the cut is always above the water table.

Cut the soil for paths on a gentle slope, using the surplus to fill the rock garden but keeping the topsoil above the subsoil. To do this, mark out the paths with long stakes and remove the topsoil from the path and the estimated high points of the rock garden to the outer regions of the construction area. Cut the subsoil from the path at the correct slope (not steeper than 1 in 15) and spread it over the estimated high points of the rock garden. Follow up by replacing the topsoil on the high points. The stakes marking the paths will have to be driven in further as work progresses, to maintain the line.

A prerequisite for this operation is a drainage system for the paths. It is best to attend to this after the paths have been cut as the drains should follow the line of the paths, out to a soakaway (if the garden has one) or to a point lower than the lowest point cut, provided that this would not interfere with other properties.

Next build the drainage system. At the lowest points in the site, build silt traps as described in Chapter Two (see figure 2) and cover each with a channel grating. Lay drainage tiles to the soakaway, or lowest point in the garden. It is not necessary to put a layer of gravel over the tiles here but if you build a soakaway use rubble and hardcore at a lower level than the drain exit and run the tiles halfway into the soakaway, which should be the same area as the ground it drains. Allowing for the heaviest storms, 10 sq m (12 sq yd) of path needs 10 cu m (14 cu yd) of soakaway. Now you can see why the site must be well above the water table.

The cut-and-fill area will add height to the finished job, so you must take this into account when estimating the amount of stone to order. The bottom layer of stones can now be laid, starting with the keystone, at the lowest point on each path. This time, when radiating outwards and up the slope, the stones will need to get progressively shorter until one end of the top surface disappears into the ground. The shallower a stone is, the longer and broader it needs to be in order to remain stable. Therefore, use stones of increasing length down the line of the path. As a stone disappears in the soil, begin the next layer with a new keystone – not necessarily in the middle as before but radiating out further each time, see figure 19. The keystone should touch the top edges of the first layer and the subsequent stones will again get shallower before they, too, perhaps disappear into the soil. Continue in this way until you reach the level of the original ground then proceed as for the single flat site.

Another alternative to leaving the path bare is to pave it using the same type of stone as for the rock garden, but note that it is not possible to pave with uneven stones such as Westmorland. The stones should never be shallower than 7 cm (3 in) unless they are bedded on a cement base, otherwise when the corners are trodden on they will dip. Lay the stone as for crazy paving. There is no need to bed any pieces thicker than 7 cm (3 in) on a cement base. The instructions for an alpine pavement given in Chapter Seven, also apply here.

Sloping Sites
Rock gardens are traditionally grown on sloping sites and if they are done well, they can look most impressive.

The steepness of slope will determine the rate of rise of stone to be laid. The greater the rise, the closer the layers of stones will be and vice versa. As with a flat site, build from the base, even if the site backs on to a wall and the temptation is to start at the top. In that instance it might be easier to use the largest stones towards the top rather than the base.

If you have a large site, access might be made easier by building a gently curving flight of steps. They should be wide enough to allow two people to pass one another, although not necessarily all the way up. Do not build steps on a small site as they reduce the planting area and can look ridiculous.

Phlox subulata *used as a crevice plant between stones.*

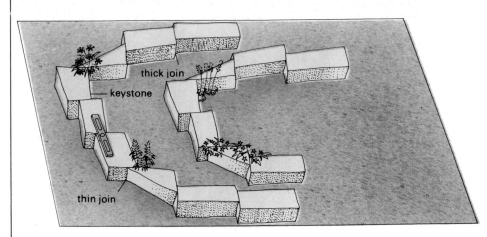

Fig. 16 A flat site, made up of several layers, each one a complete circuit. Start with a keystone and lean it backwards towards centre of site. All other stones radiate from keystone. Vary the joins between each stone, but plant during construction only in thin joins.

thick join

keystone

thin join

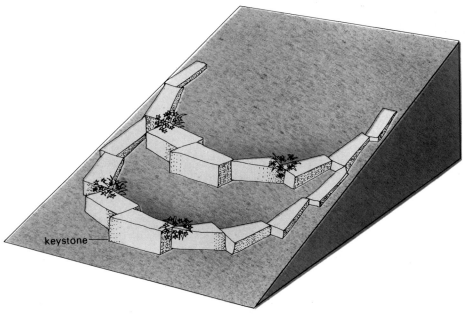

Fig. 17 A sloping site, made up of semi-circular layers. The keystone is the largest stone. Subsequent stones get progressively shallower so that they disappear into the ground at the sides of the site.

keystone

(a)

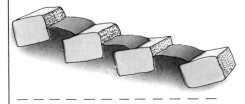

(b)

Fig. 18 (a) a rapid rise in levels and **(b)** a shallower incline. The stone is humped to allow for sinkage. The bottom of second stone is below top of first.

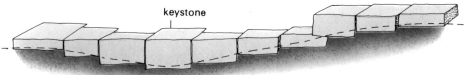

keystone

Fig. 19 (a) A cross-section of a path. Dotted line shows soil level **(b)** A plan of the path. Dotted line shows direction of path.

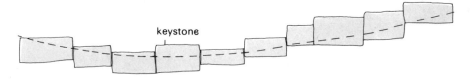

keystone

The best backdrops to a site are informal but obviously a house or outbuilding cannot be disguised. Climbers and wall shrubs can be planted to lessen the stark effect of the walls but as they create the problem of leaf fall, evergreens or even the smaller shrubs and climbers are better still.

Brick and artificial stone walls as part of a terrace are not very suitable as background but if the rock garden can be used as an expanded wall by merging the top layers of stone with the wall, so much the better. You can keep the lower bricks and blocks as long as you make drainage holes at regular intervals as the work progresses upwards. It is too risky, as well as unnecessary, to remove the wall entirely. Do not build the garden against any structure which is not already simply a retainer of soil. A house or garage wall was not designed to have soil and water above its damp course and both would eventually suffer internal damage and possible collapse.

The factors governing the design of a sloping rock garden are the same as for the flat site, except that all the layers have to 'disappear' somewhere. Informality can be best maintained by keeping any steps away from extreme ends and middle ground. Give each layer a keystone which should form the highest point for, unlike a flat site, the strata will fall gently to each side, as well as leaning back sufficiently to keep stability. Therefore, the stone will generally get shorter towards the end of the site, or else a gap will appear between the base of the upper and the lower layer (see figure 17).

There are no rules governing the steepness of steps but it is obviously easier if they are not too steep and a good guide is to make about two and a half times more tread than riser height.

To blend the steps into the layers of a rock garden, two or more steps may be made to merge into one layer, by 'bending' the steps round towards the layer. This is the only time in a rock garden that one layer of stone may be mounted on top of another successfully and with a pleasing effect, provided that not too much of the first stone is obscured.

To overcome a steep rise in the slope, take the steps round the line of contour, or even angle them.

Planting

The success of any construction lies in the plants it supports. Some plants will die, perhaps some will grow poorly but the majority should be simple and pleasurable to maintain and above all teach you, by trial and error, just what will grow in the climate, soil and situation provided for them.

The time scale I am working to in this book is 15 years. After that time, many plants will need replacing and the soil in the upper 30 cm (1 ft) will need renewing. If this is done in stages, a section at a time, then major replanting can be planned to fit in with other garden work. Unfortunately many rock gardens are merely constructed and planted and then forgotten. But they simply will not stand neglect and any design you contemplate will require regular and consistent maintenance. This factor more than any other will determine the ultimate size of the project and, as will be realised from the preceding text, cannot be taken lightly.

Instructions for planting alpines on steps and paths are given in Chapter Seven but I will mention here that where it is carried out, the soil under the stone steps and paths must have the same ingredients as that used for the rock garden and must not be left as subsoil, as recommended for the flat site and cut-and-fill paths. Getting rid of extra subsoil and replacing it with good soil and ensuring good drainage before planting means a lot of extra work.

For all path sites, it is best to plant with mat types as the steps or path stones are laid. For bare soil paths you are limited to thymes and *Saxifraga apiculata* (see table) as these can be walked on but be careful that when weeding your feet do not twist the plants as you move over the ground.

Stocking the Garden

It is difficult to estimate the number of plants required for a rock garden, but as a rough guide on each stratum put one plant per 1–3 sq metres (1–3 sq yd) of rock face, depending on the ultimate size of the plant and on what flowering plants are on the layer above. Therefore it is important to estimate the number spreading and flowing over the edges of stones as well as those to be planted at each level. Arrange small plants in loose groupings, large ones singly, and intermediate-sized plants between the two groups, with large enough spacings between to prevent the swamping of the smaller by the larger plants.

When planting on the flat surfaces of the soil between the layers of stones, you can increase the density but the principle of not swamping the smaller by larger plants still applies. Do not leave any roots exposed, nor plant deeper than the plant was either in its container or in its natural habitat. Plant firmly but not too hard, otherwise the roots will not be able to breathe.

New plantings look ridiculously sparse to start with but within two or three years, the spaces will begin to fill up.

Have a look at as many nurseries as possible, over the whole year; browse through the catalogues and seed lists before, during and after construction. It is very pleasurable to be able to fill a few reserve spaces with plants you have not come across before. Do not be afraid to uproot a few plants to make room for new and better plants, so do not grow too many vigorous plants! If possible renew the soil when replanting to maintain vigour.

The principles outlined here also apply to the remaining chapters on different aspects of alpine and rock gardening.

The majority of plants in the following table can be grown in a rock garden because of the variety of mini-habitats it can contain; my objective has been to show that although the scale and construction of other sites is different, they still provide similar growing conditions for plants as a rock garden.

Plants will show local variations in hardiness, but these will not necessarily be reflected in their temperature range. Cold combined with wet conditions can be more damaging than cold, dry ones. Flowering times will also vary according to locality. Some of the plants will not live for ten years but will produce plentiful seed. The plant names follow the International Code of Nomenclature.

Table of Alpine Plants

Working with the table

Latin plant names. Some plants will not live for 10 years but seed well.	*Details of soil conditions, type of planting, position, flowers, fruit and foliage: see key.*	*Details of sun/shade, ease of growth and winter cover: see key.*	*Size: height × width (cm).*	*Number to plant.*	*Suitable sites: see key.*
Abies balsamea hudsonia	**A CO ME FO:** *dark green*	○*	20×20	1	**R Rb Sc P S**
Acaena 'Blue Haze'	**D-ME FO:** *blue/grey.* **FR:** *red*	○*	10×2m	1	**R Rb Sc P**
Acer japonicum 'Aureum'	**A ME S FO:** *gold/green*	◠**	60×45	1	**R L**
A. palmatum 'Dissectum'	**A ME S FO:** *feathery*	◠**	40×40	1	**R L**

Key to symbols

FL – flowers: colour and time of year
FO – foliage plants, colour
FR – fruiting plant, colour of fruit (in autumn/winter)
CO – conifer
D – well-drained conditions
ME – average drainage conditions, but not too dry
W – permanently wet conditions
CU – cushion plant
MA – mat-forming plant

A – acid conditions essential
L – limestone conditions preferable, but not essential (Where no code for A & L appears, both conditions are suitable)
CR – crevice plant
SP – spring planting preferable

T – trailing plant for level ground or vertical face
B – bulb, corm or storage organ, dying down in summer unless otherwise stated
H – herbaceous perennial, dying down in winter
S – shrub
▱ – cover with sheet of glass in winter unless planted vertically
○ – sunny situation essential

● – shady situation essential
◠ – average conditions, part sun, part shade
* – easy to grow
** – harder to grow
*** – can be difficult to grow

Ready Reckoner
2.5cm – 1 inch
30cm – 1 foot
1 metre – 39 inches

Abies balsamea hudsonia	**A CO ME FO:** *dark green*	○*	20×20	1	**R Rb Sc P S**
Acaena 'Blue Haze'	**D-ME FO:** *blue/grey.* **FR:** *red*	○*	10×2m	1	**R Rb Sc P**
Acer japonicum 'Aureum'	**A ME S FO:** *gold/green*	◠**	60×45	1	**R L**
A. palmatum 'Dissectum'	**A ME S FO:** *feathery*	◠**	40×40	1	**R L**
A. palmatum 'Dissectum Atropurpureum'	**A ME S FO:** *feathery/red*	◠**	40×40	1	**R L**
Achillea clavenae (argentea)	**CR D H FL:** *white/summer.* **FO:** *grey*	○**	15×20	1	**R Rb Sc P S**
Adiantum pedatum	**A CR SP D-ME FL:** *white/summer.* **FO:** *fern*	●*	10×25	3	**R Rb P**
Adonis vernalis	**ME H FL:** *yellow.* **FO:** *feathery*	○◠*	25×25	3	**R Rb Sc**
Aethionema 'Warley Rose'	**D S FL:** *pink/summer*	○*	15×15	1	**R Rb Sc P S**
Allium beesianum	**D B FL:** *blue/July*	○*	30×10	5	**R Rb Sc**
A. narcissiflorum	**D B FL:** *purple/pink/July*	○*	25×8	5	**R Rb Sc S**
Alyssum saxatile 'Gold Dust'	**D T FL:** *yellow/May*	○*	30×45	1	**R Rb Sc**
Anacyclus depressus	**ME MA FL:** *white/red/spring & summer*	○*	8×30	1	**R Rb Sc P**
Anagallis tenella 'Studland'	**A W T FL:** *pink/July–August*	○**	3×40	1	**R Rb**
Anchusa caespitosa	**L C R SP D FL:** *blue/May–August*	○***	10×25	1	**R Rb Sc**
Androsace -arnea	**L CR SP D CU FL:** *pink/June–July*	○**	8×10	3	**R Rb Sc P S**
A. lanuginosa	**L CR SP D T FL:** *pink/July*	○**	8×30	1	**R Rb Sc P S**
A. pyrenaica	**L CR SP D CU FL:** *white/May*	○**	8×10	3	**R Rb Sc P S**
A. sarmentosa 'Salmon's Variety'	**L CR SP D T FL:** *pink/May*	○**	8×30	1	**R Rb Sc P S**
Anemone blanda 'Atrocaerulea'	**CR ME B FL:** *blue/Feb.–March*	◠*	10×20	3	**R Rb Sc L**
A. b. 'Radar'	**CR ME B FL:** *red/Feb.–March*	◠*	10×20	3	**R Rb Sc L**
Antennaria dioica	**CR ME MA SE FL:** *pink/June.* **FO:** *green*	○*	8×35	1	**R Rb Sc P S**
Anthemis marschalliana (bierbersteinii)	**CR D SE FL:** *yellow/May–June.* **FO:** *grey*	○*	20×30	1	**R Rb Sc**
Anthyllis hermanniae	**ME S FL:** *yellow/June*	○**	60×25	1	**R Rb Sc P**
Aquilegia bertolonii	**CR D H FL:** *blue/May–June*	◠**	15×10	3	**R Rb Sc S**
A. discolor	**CR D H FL:** *blue & white/May–June*	◠**	8×8	3	**R Rb Sc S**
A. flabellata	**D H FL:** *purple or white/May–June*	◠*	40×20	1	**R Rb Sc**
A. pumila (japonica)	**D H FL:** *violet & cream/April*	◠*	25×10	3	**R Rb Sc S**
Arabis ferdinandi-coburgii	**CR ME CU FO:** *green & cream*	◠**	5×25	1	**R Rb Sc S**
Arenaria balearica	**CR ME CU FL:** *white/June*	●*	2×30	3	**R Rb P**
A. montana	**CR D-ME T FL:** *white/April/May*	○*	25×40	1	**R Rb Sc**

Species	Details		Size		Propagation
Armeria juniperifolia (caespitosa)	**CR D CU FL**: *pink–white/June*	○*	15×25	1	**R Rb Sc P S**
A. maritima	**D CU FL**: *pink/May–July*	○*	25×45	1	**R Rb Sc P**
Artemisia pedemontana (assoana)	**CR SP D H CU FO**: *silver & feathery*	○*	15×30	1	**R Rb Sc P S**
A. schmidtiana Nana	**CR SP D H FO**: *silver & feathery*	○*	20×35	1	**R Rb Sc P**
Asarina procumbens	**CR SP D T FL**: *yellow/June*	●*	8×50	3	**R Rb P**
Asperula suberosa	**CR SP CU T D H FL**: *pink/May–June*	◓**	4×20	3	**R Rb Sc P S**
Aster natalense Felicia rosulata	**CR ME MA H FL**: *mauve/summer*	○*	15×30	1	**R Rb Sc**
Astilbe chinensis 'Pumila'	**ME W H FL**: *purple/July*. **FO**: *feathery*	○◓**	20×15	3	**R Rb**
A. simplicifolia (Hort)	**H ME-W FL**: *white/June*. **FO**: *feathery*	◓**	30×20	3	**R Rb**
Aubrieta hybrids	**CR ME T FL**: *mauve–red/April*	○*	15×60	1	**R Rb Sc P**
Azorella glabaria (Bolax gummifer)	**CR ME-W MA FL**: *yellow/June*. **FO**: *hard green rosettes*. **FR**: *red*	○◓*	10×40	3	**R Rb Sc P S**
Berberis thunbergii 'Atropurpurea Nana'	**ME S FL**: *yellow/spring*. **FO**: *purple*	○*	45×45	1	**R Sc**
Blechnum penna-marina	**A CR ME MA FO**: *fern*	◓●*	10×40	1	**R Rb P**
Bupleurum angulosum	**ME H FL**: *seagreen/June*. **FO**: *glaucous*	○*	30×15	3	**R Rb Sc**
Campanula carpatica 'Turbinata'	**CR D-ME H MA FL**: *blue/June–July*	○*	15×40	1	**R Rb Sc**
C. garganica	**CR D-ME H MA FL**: *violet/June–July*	○*	10×35	1	**R Rb Sc**
C. portenschlagiana	**CR D-ME H T FL**: *mauve/July–August*	○◓*	15×45	1	**R Rb Sc S**
C. pulla	**CR ME H FL**: *violet/blue/June*	○*	10×40	1	**R Rb Sc**
Cassiope mertensiana gracilis	**A CR ME S FL**: *white/May–June*	◓**	5×25	1	**R Rb Sc P S**
C. lycopodioides	**A CR ME S FL**: *white/May–June*	◓**	5×25	1	**R Rb Sc P S**
C. 'Muirhead'	**A CR ME S FL**: *white/May–June*	◓**	25×20	1	**R Rb Sc P S**
Ceratostigma plumbaginoides	**CR ME S FL**: *blue/Aug.–Sept.* **FO**: *autumn colours*	○*	30×40	1	**R Rb**
Chamaecyparis lawsoniana 'Nana Argentea'	**CO ME S FO**: *golden*	○*	30×20	1	**R Rb Sc P L S**
Chamaecyparis obtusa 'Nana Gracilis'	**CO ME S FO**: *green*	○*	10×10	1	**CR Rb Sc P L S**
Chamaepericlymenum (Cornus) canadense	**A CR ME FL**: *white/summer*. **FR**: *red*	●*	15×1m	1	**R Rb**
Chiastophyllum (Cotyledon) oppositifolium	**CR ME T FL**: *yellow/June–July*	○*	15×160	1	**R Rb**
Chionodoxa luciliae	**ME B FL**: *blue & white/March–April*	○◓*	22×8	5	**R Rb Sc L**
Clematis alpina	**CR ME T FL**: *mauve/April–May*. **SE**: *fluffy*	◓*	8×2m	1	**R Rb**
Codonopsis clematidea	**CR D-ME T H FL**: *blue/June–July*	○*	35×45	1	**R Rb**
Colchicum agrippinum	**FL**: *rose/purple/white/autumn*	◓**	30×40	10	**L**
Colchicum speciosum	**ME B FL**: *lilac/autumn*	◓**	30×40	10	**L**
Convolvulus althaeoides	**L CR SP D H T FL**: *pink/June–Aug.* **FO**: *silver*	○*	10×60	1	**R Rb Sc**
C. sabatius (mauritanicus)	**L CR D H T FL**: *blue/July*	○**	20×45	1	**R Rb Sc P S**
Coprosma petriei	**CR ME MA FO**: *dark-green*. **FR**: *purple*	○◓*	5×45	1	**R Rb Sc P S**
Cotoneaster adpressus	**CR ME S FL**: *white/April*. **FR**: *red*	○◓*	20×70	1	**R Rb Sc P**
C. horizontalis Variegatus	**CR ME S FL**: *white/April*. **FO**: *variegated* **FR**: *red*	○◓*	20×60	1	**R Rb Sc P**
C. microphyllus cochleatus	**CR ME S T FL**: *white/April*. **FR**: *red*	○◓*	15×30	1	**R Rb Sc P**
C. microphyllus thymifolius	**CR ME S MA FL**: *white/April*. **FO**: *glossy* **FR**: *red*	○◓**	5×20	1	**R Rb Sc P S**
Crocus chrysanthus hybrids	**D-ME B FL**: *various/Feb.–March*	○*	10×15	5	**R Rb Sc P L**
C. nudiflorus	**FL**: *purple/autumn*	○◓*	15×10	10	**L**
C. sieberi hybrids	**D-ME B FL**: *various/Feb.–March*	○*	15×15	5	**R Rb Sc P L**
C. tomassinianus	**D-ME FL**: *mauve/Jan.–Feb.*	○*	15×10	5	**R Rb Sc P L**
Cyananthus microphyllus	**CR ME H FL**: *blue/June–July*	○*	5×30	3	**R Rb Sc**
Cyathodes colensoi	**A ME S FL**: *white/May–June*. **FO**: *purple* **FR**: *red*	●◓**	20×20	1	**R Rb Sc P**
Cyclamen cilicium	**CR ME B FL**: *pink or white/Sept.–Oct.* **SE**: *coils*	●◓**	8×10	5	**R Rb P L S**
C. coum	**CR ME B FL**: *pink or white/Dec.–Jan.* **SE**: *coils*	●◓*	8×10	5	**R Rb P L S**
C. hederifolium (neapolitanum)	**CR ME B FL**: *pink or white/Aug.–Oct.* **FO**: *ivy-leaved* **SE**: *coils*	●◓*	12×30	5	**R Rb P L**
C. repandum	**CR ME B FL**: *pink/March–May*. **FO**: *ivy-leaved* **SE**: *coils*	●◓**	10×10	5	**R Rb Sc P L S**
Cytisus ardoinii	**CR D-ME S T FL**: *yellow/May*	○*	15×40	1	**R Rb Sc P**

Name	Description	Symbol	Size	No.	Codes
C. demissus	**CR D-ME T FL:** *cream/May–June*	○*	5×35	1	**R Rb Sc P**
C. kewensis	**CR D-ME S FL:** *cream/May*	○*	30×1m	1	**R Rb Sc P**
Daphne alpinum	**D-ME S FL:** *white (scented)/May*	○*	30×20	1	**R Rb Sc P S**
D. cneorum 'Eximea'	**CR D-ME S T FL:** *pink (scented)/May*	○**	15×45	1	**R Rb Sc**
D. retusa	**ME S FL:** *rose/purple/white (scented)/ May*	○**	35×35	1	**R Rb Sc P**
Delphinium tatsienense	**CR D-ME H FL:** *blue/summer*	○**	35×15	3	**R Rb Sc**
Dianthus alpinus	**CR D CU FL:** *pink/red/summer*	○*	8×20	3	**R Rb Sc S**
D. amurensis	**CR D S FL:** *mauve/summer*	○*	15×35	3	**R Rb Sc**
D. 'Pike's Pink'	**CR D S FL:** *pink/summer.* **FO:** *blue/grey*	○*	20×1m	1	**R Rb Sc**
Diascia 'Ruby Field'	**CR D H FL:** *salmon/summer*	○**	20×30	1	**R Rb Sc**
Dicentra formosa oregana	**CR D-ME H FL:** *red/May.* **FO:** *blue/grey*	○◠*	25×1m	1	**R Rb Sc**
Dodecatheon pulchellum 'Red Wings'	**D-ME-W H FL:** *red/April–May*	○◠*	20×15	3	**R Rb Sc P**
Doronicum cordatum	**D-ME H FL:** *yellow/Feb.–April*	○*	25×1m	1	**R**
Draba rigida bryoides	**L CR CU FL:** *yellow/March–April*	○**	3×15	3	**R Rb Sc P S**
Dryas octopetala	**CR D-ME MA FL:** *white/June (fluffy seeds)*	○*	15×1m	1	**R Rb Sc P**
Edraianthus pumilio	**CR D CU H FL:** *blue/June.* **FO:** *blue grey*	○**	8×20	1	**R Rb Sc P S**
Eranthis hyemalis	**D-ME D FL:** *yellow/Jan.–March*	○◠*	10×10	5	**R Rb Sc P L**
Erica carnea 'Springwood Pink'	**A CR ME S FL:** *pink/Dec.–Feb.*	○◠*	20×60	1	**R**
E. c. 'Springwood White'	**A CR ME S FL:** *white/Dec.–Feb.*	○◠*	20×60	1	**R**
E. c. vivellii	**A CR ME S FL:** *wine/Dec.–Feb.* **FO:** *dark green*	○◠*	20×60	1	**R**
Erigeron aureus	**CR D-ME H FL:** *yellow/spring–summer*	○*	10×15	1	**R Rb Sc S**
Erinacea antyllis	**CR D S FL:** *blue/April*	○**	25×25	1	**R Rb Sc P S**
Erinus alpinus	**CR D CU FL:** *pink/white/April–May*	○*	8×12	3	**R Rb Sc P S**
Erodium corsicum	**CR D MA FL:** *pink/May–Sept.*	○**	10×20	1	**R Rb Sc P S**
E. reichardii (chamaedrioides)	**CR D MA FL:** *pink–white/April–Sept.* **FO:** *grey/green*	○**	10×15	1	**R Rb Sc P S**
Eryngium alpinum	**D H FL:** *blue & white/summer*	○*	45×30	1	**R Rb Sc**
E. bourgattii	**D H FL:** *blue/summer*	○*	45×30	1	**R Rb Sc**
Erythronium dens-canis	**ME B FL:** *rose/April.* **FO:** *mottled*	●◠*	15×25	5	**R Rb S L**
E. tuolumnense	**ME B FL:** *yellow/April*	◠*	30×15	5	**R Rb L**
Euphorbia myrsinites	**CR D T FL:** *yellow green/June–July* **FO:** *blue/grey*	○*	16×60	1	**R Rb Sc**
Festuca ovina glauca	**CR D FO:** *blue-grey (grass)*	○*	15×30	1	**R Rb Sc P**
F. glacialis	**CR D FO:** *blue-grey (grass)*	○*	10×12	1	**R Rb Sc P S**
Fritillaria meleagris	**ME-W B FL:** *purple or yellow/May*	○◠*	20×15	5	**R Sc P L**
Fuchsia 'Alice Hoffman'	**ME S FL:** *red & white/summer*	◠*	25×15	1	**R Rb**
F. magellanica 'Versicolor'	**ME S FL:** *scarlet & violet/summer* **FO:** *variegated*	◠*	60×60	1	**R Rb**
F. 'Pumila'	**ME S FL:** *scarlet & violet/summer*	◠*	25×20	1	**R Rb Sc**
F. 'Tom Thumb'	**ME S FL:** *scarlet & violet/summer*	◠*	15×15	1	**R Rb Sc**
Galanthus nivalis	**ME B FL:** *white/Jan.–March*	●◠*	15×15	5	**R Rb Sc P L**
G. n. reginae-olgae	**ME B FL:** *white/Nov.*	●◠*	10×12	5	**R Rb Sc P L**
Gaultheria cuneata	**A CR ME FL:** *white/June.* **FR:** *white*	●◠*	25×40	1	**R Rb P**
G. miqueliana	**A ME FL:** *white-pink/June.* **FR:** *white/July*	●◠*	30×60	1	**R Rb P**
G. procumbens	**A CR ME FL:** *white.* **FO:** *red/green.* **FR:** *red*	●◠*	16×60	1	**R Rb P**
Genista pilosa	**CR D-ME S FL:** *yellow/May–June*	○*	30×45	1	**R Rb Sc**
G. lydia	**CR D-ME FL:** *yellow/May–June*	○*	30×60	1	**R Rb Sc P**
Gentiana acaulis	**CR L D ME MA FL:** *blue/spring.* **FO:** *glossy*	○**	8×20	3	**R Rb Sc P S**
G. septemfida	**ME H FL:** *blue/June*	○◠*	20×20	1	**R Rb**
G. sino-ornata	**A ME H FL:** *blue/Oct.–Dec.*	○◠**	10×15	3	**R Rb S**
G. verna	**L D-ME FL:** *blue/April–May.* **FO:** *shiny*	○**	6×12	3	**R Rb Sc P S**
Geranium cinereum 'Ballerina'	**CR D MA H FL:** *pink/summer*	○*	10×25	1	**R Rb Sc**
G. sanguineum lancastriense	**CR D H FL:** *salmon/summer*	○*	10×40	1	**R Rb Sc**
Haberlea rhodopensis	**CR ME FL:** *mauve/May–June.* **FO:** *leathery*	●*	10×15	1	**R Rb P S**
H. r. 'Virginalis'	**CR ME FL:** *white/May–June.* **FO:** *leathery*	●*	10×15	1	**R Rb P S**
Hakonechloa macra 'Aureola'	**ME H FO:** *golden (grass)*	●◠*	30×30	1	**R Rb**

Name	Description	Symbol	Size	No.	Codes
Hebe 'Carl Teschner'	**D-ME S FL:** *mauve/July–August*	○*	20×40	1	**R Rb Sc P**
H. pagei	**D-ME S FL:** *white/July–August*	○*	20×40	1	**R Rb Sc P**
Hedera helix 'Goldheart'	**D-ME T FO:** *variegated (Ivy)*	○◠*	5×1m	1	**R Rb P**
Helianthemum 'Amy Baring'	**D-ME S FL:** *orange/June*	○*	10×35	1	**R Rb Sc P**
H. nummularium grandiflorum	**D-ME S FL:** *yellow/June*	○*	15×30	1	**R Rb Sc P S**
H. 'Wisley Primrose'	**D-ME S FL:** *pink/June.* **FO:** *grey*	○*	15×1m	1	**R Rb Sc P**
Helichrysum frigidum	**CR D CU FL:** *white/summer.* **FO:** *grey*	○**	5×15	3	**R Rb Sc P S**
Hepatica nobilis (triloba)	**A ME H FL:** *blue, red or white*	●◠**	10×20	3	**R Rb**
Hutchinsia alpina	**D-ME CU FL:** *white/June–July*	○*	5×45	1	**R Rb Sc P**
Hypericum aegypticum	**D-ME S FL:** *yellow/summer.* **FO:** *grey/green*	○*	20×20	1	**R Rb Sc P S**
H. olympicum	**D-ME S FL:** *yellow/June–August*	○*	25×25	1	**R Rb Sc P**
Iberis semperflorens (not to be confused with I. sempervirens)	**D-ME S FL:** *white/Oct.–Feb.*	○*	20×25	1	**R Rb Sc P**
Incarvillea 'Bee's Pink'	**ME H FL:** *pink/May–July.* **FO:** *bronze/green*	◠**	20×30	3	**R Rb**
I. compacta	**ME H FL:** *pink/May–July*	◠*	25×30	3	**R Rb**
I. delavayi	**ME H FL:** *rose/May–July*	◠*	70×40	3	**R**
Iris innominata hybrids	**ME FL:** *yellow-brown/June–July*	○*	25×35	1	**R Sc P**
I. lacustris	**D FL:** *mauve and gold/summer*	○**	8×10	3	**R Rb Sc P S**
Jasminum parkeri	**D S T FL:** *yellow/July*	▭○◠**	10×30	1	**R Rb Sc P S**
Jeffersonia diphylla	**ME H FL:** *white/March–April*	◠**	15×20	1	**R Rb Sc**
J. dubia	**ME H FL:** *lilac/March–April.* **FO:** *bronze*	◠**	20×20	1	**R Rb Sc**
Juniperus communis 'Compressa'	**D-ME CO FO:** *blue/green*	○*	25×7	1	**R Rb Sc P L S**
J. c. 'Hornibrokii'	**D-ME CO T FO:** *dark green*	○*	8×35	1	**R Rb Sc P L S**
J. c. repanda	**D-ME CO T FO:** *light green*	○*	15×1m	1	**R L**
J. chinensis 'Echiniformis'	**CR D-ME CO MA FO:** *glaucous*	○***	8×10	1	**R Rb S P L S**
J. conferta	**D-ME CO MA FO:** *apple green*	○*	30×1m	1	**R L**
J. horizontalis 'Bar Harbor'	**D-ME CO TR FO:** *glaucous*	○*	20×1.5m	1	**R Sc L**
J. 'Pfitzeriana Aurea'	**CO D FO:** *golden*	○*	1×2m	1	**L**
J. sabina tamariscifolia	**D T CO FO:** *grey*	○*	6×1.5m	1	**L**
J. virginiana 'Grey Owl'	**CO D T FO:** *blue/grey*	○*	20×1.5m	1	**L**
Lavandula stoechas	**D S FL:** *violet/summer.* **FO:** *grey*	○*	40×40	1	**R Rb Sc P**
Leucojum autumnale	**D B FL:** *white & pink/Sept.–Oct.*	○*	8×4	10	**R Rb Sc P L**
Leontopodium alpinum	**CR D H FL:** *white & yellow/May–July;* **FO:** *grey*	○**	15×15	1	**R Rb Sc**
Leucojum aestivum 'Gravetye'	**ME-W B FL:** *white & green/May*	○◠*	40×20	3	**L**
Leucojum vernum	**ME-W B FL:** *white & green/March*	◠*	30×20	3	**L**
Lewisia cotyledon hybrids	**A CR D FL:** *pink/May*	▭◠**	25×15	3	**R Rb Sc S**
L. tweedyi	**CR D FL:** *salmon/May (vertical planting best)*	▭◠***	15×20	1	**R Rb Sc P**
Limonium caesium	**CR D CU H FL:** *pink/summer-autumn*	○*	25×15	1	**R Rb Sc P S**
Linum flavum	**D S FL:** *yellow/summer*	○**	45×20	1	**R Rb Sc P S**
Lithodora (Lithospermum) diffusa 'Heavenly Blue'	**A CR SP S D T FL:** *blue/summer*	○**	15×1.5m	1	**R Rb Sc**
Lysimachia nummularia 'Aurea'	**ME-W T FL:** *yellow/June.* **FO:** *yellow*	○◠*	5×1m	1	**R Rb**
Margyricarpus setosus	**CR D S T FL:** *green/summer.* **FR:** *semi-translucent*	○**	15×40	1	**R Rb Sc P**
Mazus reptans	**CR D CU FL:** *rosy lavender, white & brown/May–Oct.*	○**	2×40	1	**R Rb Sc P S**
Morisia monanthos hypogea	**CR D-ME CU FL:** *yellow/March–April*	○**	4×10	3	**R Rb Sc P S**
Narcissus asturiensis (minimus)	**D B FL:** *yellow/Feb.–March*	○*	5×4	10	**R Rb Sc P L S**
N. bulbocodium	**D-ME B FL:** *yellow/March–April*	○◠*	15×5	5	**R Rb Sc P L S**
N. cyclamineus	**ME-W B FL:** *yellow/March*	○◠**	15×5	5	**R Rb P L**
N. triandrus albus	**D B FL:** *white/April*	○◠*	15×8	5	**R Rb Sc P L S**
Nerine bowdenii	**D B FL:** *pink/late summer-autumn*	○**	45×20	1	**R Rb Sc P**
Nierembergia repens (rivularis)	**CR ME-W MA FL:** *white/summer*	○**	2×40	1	**R Rb P**
Nomocharis mairei	**A ME H FL:** *white, spotted red/June–July*	●**	50×30	1	**R Rb**
Oenothera mi-souriensis	**CR D H T FL:** *yellow/summer*	○*	15×1m	1	**R**
Origanum scabrum	**CR D S FL:** *pink & green/summer*	○**	10×30	1	**R Rb Sc S**
Oxalis adenophora	**CR D B FL:** *pink/May–June.* **FO:** *glaucous*	○***	8×10	3	**R Rb Sc S**

Name	Description	Symbol	Size	No.	Codes
Papaver fauriei miyabeanum	**CR D H FL:** *yellow/summer.* **FO:** *light-green hairy (treat as annual).* **FR:** *brown*	○**	12×30	3	**R Rb Sc**
Parochetus communis	**A ME-W T FL:** *blue/Nov.–Jan. (not in cold areas)*	●◠**	10×1m	1	**R**
Penstemon davidsonii	**CR D S FL:** *red/June–July*	○***	15×20	1	**R Rb Sc P S**
P. pinifolius	**CR D S FL:** *scarlet/June–July*	○*	25×35	1	**R Rb Sc P**
P. scouleri	**CR D S FL:** *lilac/May–June*	○**	20×25	1	**R Rb Sc P S**
Philadelphus 'Manteau d'Hermoine'	**ME S FL:** *white (scented)/June*	○*	60×60	1	**R P L**
Phlox douglasii 'May Snow'	**CR D MA FL:** *white/May–June*	○*	10×60	1	**R Rb Sc P**
P. d. 'Rosea'	**CR D MA FL:** *pink/May–June*	○*	10×60	1	**R Rb Sc P**
P. subulata 'G. F. Wilson'	**CR D MA FL:** *lilac/May–June*	○*	15×1m	1	**R Rb Sc P**
P. s. 'Temiscaming'	**CR D MA FL:** *crimson/May–June*	○*	15×1m	1	**R Rb Sc P**
Physoplexis (Phyteuma) comosa	**L CR SP D H FL:** *blue & white/July*	▢○◠***	10×15	3	**R Rb Sc S**
Picea abies 'Gregoriana'	**D CO FO:** *medium green*	○*	15×25	1	**R Rb Sc P S**
P. mariana 'Nana'	**D CO FO:** *glaucous*	○*	20×25	1	**R Rb Sc P S**
Pinus mugo 'Mops'	**D CO FO:** *dark green*	○*	35×35	1	**R Rb Sc P S**
P. sylvestris 'Beuvronensis'	**D CO FO:** *grey-green*	○*	30×30	1	**R Rb Sc P S**
Platycodon grandiflorum	**D H FL:** *blue/July–Sept.*	○**	30×15	3	**R Rb Sc**
Podocarpus alpinus	**D CO T FO:** *medium green*	○*	15×30	1	**R Rb Sc P S**
Polygala chamaebuxus	**ME-W S T FL:** *red/yellow/April–June*	○◠*	15×30	1	**R Rb Sc S**
Polygonum affine 'Darjeeling Red'	**CR ME-W MA T FL:** *red/Aug.–Oct.* **FO:** *aut. col.*	○◠*	20×1m	1	**R Rb Sc P**
P. vaccinifolium	**CR ME-W S T FL:** *pink/Sept.–Oct.*	●◠*	15×1m	1	**R Rb P**
Potentilla aurea	**CR D S FL:** *yellow/summer*	○*	10×35	1	**R Rb Sc P**
P. cuneata (eriocarpa)	**CR ME FL:** *yellow/June–July*	○*	5×35	1	**R Rb Sc P**
P. fruticosa 'Elizabeth'	**D-ME S MA FL:** *yellow/summer*	○*	20×60	1	**R Rb Sc P**
P. 'Tonguei'	**CR D-ME S T FL:** *orange/summer*	○*	5×1m	1	**R Rb Sc**
Primula auricula hybrids	**CR D FL:** *white or yellow (not florist types)/spring–summer*	○**	8×20	1	**R Rb Sc S**
P. farinosa	**ME H FL:** *mauve/April–May.* **FO:** *mealy*	◠**	7×10	3	**R Rb Sc S**
P. frondosa	**ME H FL:** *mauve/May.* **FO:** *mealy*	◠*	10×15	1	**R Rb Sc S**
P. juliae	**ME H FL:** *pink/March–April.* **FO:** *deep bronze*	●◠*	6×10	3	**R Rb S**
P x marginata	**CR D FL:** *mauve-blue*	○*	8×15	1	**R Rb Sc P S**
P. minima	**CR SP D FL:** *pink/April–May*	○◠***	6×12	3	**R Rb Sc P S**
P x pubescens	**CR SP D FL:** *various colours/spring*	○**	10×12	3	**R Rb Sc P S**
P. vialii	**ME H FL:** *mauve and pink/May–June*	●◠**	60×20	3	**R**
Prunella grandiflora 'Loveliness'	**ME MA FL:** *lavender/summer*	○◠*	15×1m	1	**R Sc P**
Ptilotrichum (Alyssum) spinosum 'Roseum'	**D S FL:** *pink/June* **FO:** *spiky effect with stems*	○**	20×20	1	**R Rb Sc P S**
Pulsatilla (Anemone) halleri slavica	**D H FL:** *hairy pink/June*	○**	15×20	1	**R Rb Sc**
P(a) vernalis	**ME H FL:** *purple & white, hairy/May*	○◠***	15×15	3	**R Rb**
P(a) vulgaris	**ME-D H FL:** *purple/April*	○*	30×30	1	**R Rb Sc**
Punica granatum 'Nana'	**D S FL:** *scarlet/June–Aug.*	○***	15×15	1	**R Rb Sc P S'**
Ramonda myconi	**CR ME FL:** *mauve/June.* **FO:** *leathery*	●**	10×25	3	**R Rb S**
Raoulia hookeri	**D CU FO:** *silver*	▢○**	2×30	1	**R Rb Sc P S**
R. tenuicaulis	**D CU FO:** *dark green*	○**	2×60	1	**R Rb Sc P S**
Rhododendron calostrotum	**A CR ME S MA FL:** *magenta/May–June* **FO:** *grey/green*	◠*	20×30	1	**R Rb P L S**
R. 'Elizabeth'	**A ME S MA FL:** *large red/April* **FO:** *large dark*	◠*	15×45	1	**R Rb P L**
R. ferrugineum	**A CR ME S MA FL:** *crimson, June* **FO:** *rusty underneath*	◠*	20×30	1	**R Rb Sc P L S**
R. impeditum	**A CR ME S FL:** *purple, April/May*	○◠*	15×20	1	**R Rb Sc P L S**
R. keleticum	**A CR ME S MA FL:** *purple/May–June* **FO:** *dark green*	◠*	15×40	1	**R Rb P L S**
R. pemakoense	**A CR ME S MA FL:** *lilac-purple/March–April*	◠*	8×30	1	**R Rb P L S**
R. russatum	**A ME S FL:** *violet & white/April–May*	○◠*	50×40	1	**R Rb L**
R. yakushimanum	**A ME S FL:** *pink–white/May* **FO:** *dark green above, brown underneath*	◠*	70×70	1	**R Rb L**
Rhodohypoxis baurii	**D B FL:** *red-pink-white/May–July*	▢○**	8×8	10	**R Rb Sc S**
Roscoea cautleoides	**A ME-W H FL:** *yellow/June–July*	◠*	45×20	3	**R**

Name	Description	Symbol	Size	No.	Codes
R. humeana	A ME-W H FL: purple/June–July	◠*	35×20	3	R Rb
Sagina glabra 'Aurea'	CR ME-W CU FO: yellow green	○*	2×30	1	R Rb P S
Salix arbuscula	CR ME-W S T FO: soft green	○*	8×50	1	R Rb P S
S. 'Boydii'	D-ME S FO: grey furry	○**	15×15	1	R Rb P S
Sanguinaria canadensis 'Plena'	A CR ME H FL: white/April	●◠**	25×25	1	R Rb
Saponaria ocymoides	CR D-ME MA FL: pink purple/summer	○*	10×60	1	R Rb Sc P
Sarococca humilis	A ME S FL: white (scented)/January FO: dark green. FR: black	●*	15×25	1	R Rb P
Saxifraga x apiculata	CR L D CU FL: yellow/March. FO: dense green	○*	5×30	1	R Rb Sc P S
S. cochlearis 'Minor'	CR L D CU FL: white/March. FO: dense blue/grey	○*	15 cm flower 3cm foliage	10	R Rb Sc P S
S. fortunei	A CR ME-W H FL: white/Sept.–Nov. FO: bronze	◠*	20×25	1	R Rb
S. oppositifolia	L CR D CU FL: pink/March. FO: dense green	○**	5×20	1	R Rb Sc P S
S. paniculata baldensis	L CR D CU FL: white/May. FO: dense grey/blue	○*	3×40	1	R Rb Sc P S
S. 'Tumbling Waters'	L CR D FL: white/June Monocarpic flowers after about six years then max. size	▱○**	60×25	1	R Rb Sc P S
S. 'Southside Seedling'	L CR D FL: white, and pink spots/May–June	○*	40×15 inc. fl.	1	R Rb Sc P S
S. 'Winston Churchill'	CR ME-W FL: red/April–June	●◠*	10×60	1	R Rb P
Schizostylis coccinea 'Sunrise'	ME-W FL: pink/Oct.–Dec.	○*	40×15	3	R Rb Sc P
Scilla sibirica	D-ME B FL: blue and white/February	○◠*	10×8	10	R Rb Sc P L S
Sedum cauticolum	D FL: pink/autumn. FO: purple-grey	○*	8×30	1	R Rb Sc P S
S. spathulifolium 'Cappa Blanca'	D FL: yellow/May–June. FO: silver grey	○*	8×30	1	R Rb Sc P S
S. s. 'Atropurpureum'	D FL: yellow/May–June. FO: purple	○*	8×30	1	R Rb Sc P S
Sempervivum arachnoideum	D FL: pink/summer. FO: spiders' web and red	○*	3×20	1	R Rb Sc P S
S. 'Commander Hay'	D FL: pink/summer. FO: green and maroon	○*	3×30	1	R Rb Sc P S
Sisyrinchium bermudianum	ME FL: blue/summer	○*	25×10	3	R Rb Sc P
Soldanella alpina	ME FL: deep mauve/April–May FO: round, dark green	○◠**	8×10	3	R Rb Sc S
Sorbus reducta	D-ME S FL: white/May–June FR: white, pink. FO: autumn colours	○*	45×45	1	R Rb Sc P
Spiraea x bumalda 'Nyewood'	D-ME S FL: pink/summer	○*	60×1m	1	R Rb L
Sternbergia lutea	D B FL: yellow/October	○**	10×10	1	R Rb Sc P L
Teucrium subspinosum	CR D S FL: pink/summer. FO: grey	▱○*	10×10	1	R Rb Sc P S
Thymus lanuginosus	CR D-ME MA FL: pink/June. FO: dark & hairy	○*	2×50	1	R Rb Sc P
T. praecox arcticus (serpyllum) (drucei)	CR D-ME MA FL: pink/June. FO: dark	○*	2×50	1	R Rb Sc P
Tiarella wherryi	ME H FL: white/May–June. FO: red on green	◠*	30×1m	1	R Rb
Tricyrtis hirta	ME-W H FL: white & purple/Sept.–Oct.	◠**	60×20	3	R
Trollius acaulis	ME-W H FL: yellow/May–June	○*	60×20	3	R Rb
T. pumilus	ME-W H FL: yellow/May–June	○*	20×15	3	R Rb S
Tulipa greigii hybrids	D B FL: scarlet/yellow D B FL: scarlet/yellow and black/April	○**	15×10	5	R Rb Sc P
T. kaufmanniana hybrids	D B FL: white, red or yellow/March	○**	15×10	5	R Rb Sc P
Uvularia grandiflora	A ME H FL: yellow/May	◠**	30×10	3	R Rb L
Vaccinium vitis-idaea	A ME S FL: pink or white/May–June	◠*	15×20	1	R Rb P
Verbascum 'Letitia'	D S FL: yellow FO: grey on spiky stems	○**	30×30	1	R Rb Sc P S
Veronica gentianoides	D-ME H MA FL: blue/June	○*	20×40	1	R Rb Sc P
Vinca minor 'La Grave' 'Bowles Variety'	D-ME S T FL: blue/summer	●◠*	15×80	1	R Rb P
Viola 'Haslemere'	ME H FL: pink/summer	○◠*	15×25	1	R Rb
Vitaliana (Douglasia) primuliflora praetutiana	L CR D CU FL: yellow/May–July. FO: silver grey	▱○**	4×15	3	R Rb Sc P S
Zauschneria cana	CR D T FL: scarlet/Aug.–Oct. FO: grey	○**	30×40	1	R Rb Sc P
Z. californica	CR D T FL: scarlet/Aug.–Oct.	○**	40×50	1	R Rb Sc P

Chapter five

Raised Beds

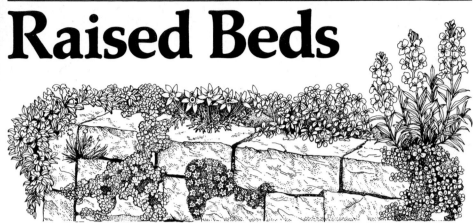

Building raised beds, alpine pavements and sink gardens offers the average gardener the greatest scope for growing alpine plants. A unique compromise between size and shape, they can fit into almost any garden space. The original number of constructions can be increased as the pocket and time allow. Do not be too ambitious to start with; a small project can be built up gradually over a period of time.

Extending the garden may particularly suit the young married couple with children – what better way of introducing youngsters to the delights of gardening than with the supervised construction and planting of their own sites? At the other end of the scale, raised beds offer the elderly the best opportunities for a degree of independence not often possible in other forms of gardening.

Almost any site, sloping or flat, in sun or shade or both, may be considered suitable for the construction of a raised bed.

Obviously those constructed from natural stone will look best, but any retaining materials can be used. Where the finances are limited (and plants are the main concern anyway) the clothing of other materials by alpine plants can be very effective and help to take away their possibly stark effect.

The easiest shape to maintain is a relatively narrow one, whose centre can be reached, without undue effort, from one or more sides at the basic ground level.

The basic requirements for prepar-

Sunny yellow alyssum and brilliant white iberis go together to make a delightful spring cover to the wall.

ing the site are the same as for the rock garden: the most important being good drainage and absence of perennial weeds. Other similarities will be mentioned later. The most important difference is that maintenance should be easy and you should not need to tread on the site after it is completed.

Materials

Taking natural stone first: this material can be used (unlike in the rock garden) in any reasonable size. It is not advisable to mix the types of stone on any one site; better to build two small sites with different types of stone than one larger one mixing the two together. Have a look at well-laid dry-stone walls surrounding some farms for inspiration.

Stones come in a variety of sizes and shapes. Do not be misled by some public gardens where you may have seen large stones used all the time; this is done deliberately to allow for misuse by the public, who insist on kicking them to see if they are strong or who simply sit on them, which dislodges the stones, one at a time. And, mindful that children will climb anything that can be climbed – either for pleasure or to retrieve toys – large stones or other building materials, may be the answer.

Apart from stone, a wide variety of materials can be used to build a raised bed: railway sleepers; bricks, particularly weathered ones; concrete, which should never be pebble-dashed or treated with a surface material to take away its stark appearance (it will chip and fall off after a cold spell); artificial stone, both formally and informally designed. Regardless of the material

used, the basic rule of no soil between each layer applies, because rain and artificial watering would gradually wash the soil away, causing the materials to dislodge and destroy the structure.

Design

There are various designs to choose from, but like the rock garden, in all cases the width will depend on the height (varying from 15 cm to 1 metre (6 in to 3 ft)) which is also relative to the length and, in turn, depends on whether the ground slopes or not.

If you build a bed 1 metre (3 ft)

high, getting up to tread on the site may not be practical, but with a long, low site, not more than 60 cm (2 ft) high, you can put in stepping stones and thus reach the centre or back areas, according to whether the site is independent or backs on to a wall. No construction should back on to a house or other wall with damp courses.

The shape of a raised bed will obviously vary according to the space available; try to avoid squares if at all possible and choose from formal rectangles, L-shapes or long curves. The spaces surrounding any site can be

The curved outline of this raised bed makes an informal retaining wall for a pretty display of alpines.

grassed, paved or left as bare soil. Where grass borders the walls, it is advisable to lay paving slabs, using the same material as the raised bed, between the grass and the site, as this makes maintenance and mowing easier. The method is described in Chapter Four, page 29. Use the same soil mixtures as for a rock garden: humus-based for shady sites, and gritty mixes for the sunny ones, see page 14.

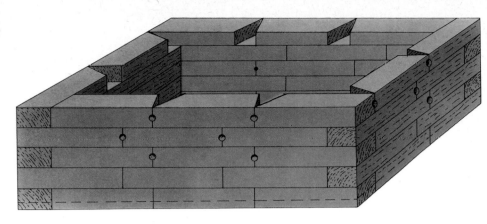

Fig. 20 Railway sleepers cut in half lengthways to reduce their depth are easier to position and afford more planting spaces. A 'V' shaped cut with a small hole in the middle provides planting spaces in the vertical joins between sleepers.

Fig. 21 Three possible designs for raised beds, **(a)** L-shaped **(b)** curved **(c)** convex on all sides.

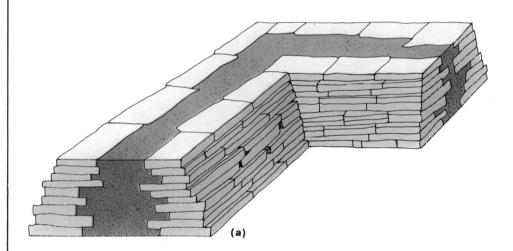

(a)

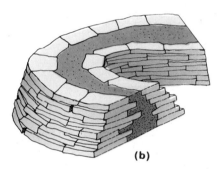

(b)

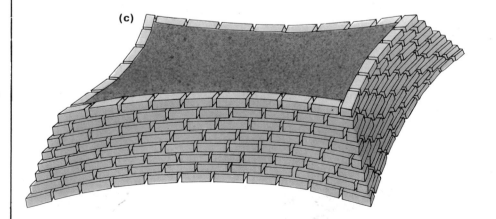

(c)

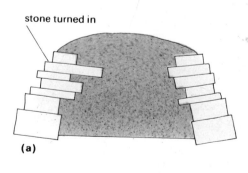

stone turned in

(a)

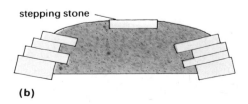

stepping stone

(b)

Fig. 22 (right) **(a)** Walls over 2 m long and 45 cm high are strengtherned with stones turned in to form buttresses.

(b) A stepping stone placed in the middle of a site not more than 60 cm high enables you to reach the back of the site.

Construction

The same construction principles as for building a rock garden apply.

The corner ends of a raised bed can be squared off or curved. Squared ends, interlocked at the sides like brickwork, are stronger but perhaps less smooth and polished-looking. Curved ends look much better and gentle sweeps are very much easier to construct.

As the work proceeds, inspect the site from different angles – not after laying every stone, but often enough to make corrections simple. This applies to a flat or sloping site.

Building Materials

The simplest construction is made from railway sleepers (beware of soft tar in the summer) sunk about 3–5 cm (1–2 in) below the ground level and leaning gently back towards the site, with the broadest surface to the ground (see figure 20). Additional layers can be added to the base using the bricklaying technique of overlapping the joints.

Bricks and artificial stone blocks may be laid the same way as sleepers but the degree of leaning needs to be greater to resist the outward pressure of the soil onto their individually smaller surface areas. The height to which such a bed can be raised is limited – because of that pressure – to a maximum of five convexly sloping layers of bricks or blocks. This shape is stronger than any other.

Another possible building material is limestone. Tufa stone, an expensive form of limestone, is unusual in that pieces can be laid to form a surface almost completely composed of stone, with a number of small areas of exposed soil for planting. It looks glaringly white when purchased, yet within two years, it takes on first a pink tinge, then becomes grey tinged with pink, making it look old and weathered in a very short time. It is particularly effective on awkward sloping sites in small gardens. Since it is a relatively light material, use pieces as large as possible placed on their edges with a slight tilt towards the slope. They may be fitted together to form any height up to 1½ metres (4½ ft). Because of the nature of the stone, do not try to build it further into the slope than can be reached from any

natural ground level. It will not take kindly to being trodden on regularly. Details for planting in tufa stone are given in Chapter Two, page 13. Avoid planting any thick, fleshy-rooted plants in the stone itself; these will do very much better if planted in the soil pockets between.

The stepping stones for any of the sites must be carefully considered. Railway sleepers will make a very stable structure, but a bed made from bricks, blocks and small stones if more than three layers high, will have stability problems. Every step made on the site will increase the outward pressure and to reduce that as much as possible, choose stones weighing not less than 11 kg (25 lb). Their surface areas should be large enough to accommodate two feet on one stone at a time and they should be close enough together to prevent you from having to leap when moving from one stone to another!

Stone-built raised beds are made by laying one stone upon another, starting just below ground level. There is no keystone so they may be built in any sequence, to left, right or upwards, to a predetermined level. Flat stones are easier to lay than rounded ones, but it is worthwhile making trial constructions to discover the possibilities of your own materials. If you have any smaller stones do not use them for the base or the top; these should be held in place by the larger stones. Short, rounded stones will dislodge easily, even when wedged between larger ones, as a trial run will bear out. The only real limit to the size of stone you can use is the size of the project itself.

Difficult joins between the stones can be overcome by placing stone wedges between the soil and the wall, but this should not be done too often or there will be a bulk of stone and not much room for the plants. An alternative solution is to use the spaces for planting.

Walls over 2 metres (6 ft) long and over 45 cm (18 in) high can be strengthened by building buttresses. To do this, simply turn some of the stones at approximately 1 metre (3 ft) intervals along the length of the wall and at varying heights, so that they

Alyssum saxatile *used as a crevice plant in a dry stone wall.*

44

lie in an opposite plane to the line of the building. With soil above and below these buttresses, some of the pressure will be eased off the wall.

The height of the completed bed must be the same to within 5 cm (2 in) throughout its length, to keep the soil within the site and not lose any through gaps on the top layer. Thus the soil is being positioned whilst building is done. This strengthens the walls and enables you to firm round the buttresses and to plant between the retaining materials. Planning and execution of planting should follow the same principles as for the rock garden.

I have left the use of concrete until last because as a material it is the exception to the rule. There are no layers, and no holes to plant in; instead, obtaining a natural effect relies entirely upon trailing and mat plants falling over the surface to reduce its harsh appearance and to break up its flatness. I would never recommend building a concrete wall specifically for this purpose, only utilizing an existing one, simply because other materials are so much better. But never use a wall that is cracked and broken, or made up of a hotch-potch of bits and pieces, because walls of this kind harbour weeds including perennials and make maintenance a drudgery. It is much better to break the wall down and start from scratch, using one of the other materials.

The drainage at the base of a concrete wall will have to be good because there is no way out through the sides. The soil should, ideally, be entirely renewed to improve further the drainage quality of soil for the alpines. There will probably be concrete foundations below ground level, often thicker than the walls they support; if the soil is clay it is best to fill the base with rubble to ensure good drainage below these foundations.

Sloping Sites

Building a raised bed on a sloping site can be compared with the more formal construction of a rock garden on a slope. The retaining materials are laid from the lowest level up-

wards, so that the height of the wall at the top of the slope is about 15 cm (6 in). The layers should be horizontal at each level. You can make a continuous run of beds if you have a large area available.

You can build on a north facing slope so as to make the flat surface of the soil face the sunlight and hence can support a greater range of plants but you must anticipate obstructions to the light in winter, when the soil lies cold and damp and the greatest loss of plants is likely to occur. Planting woodland and semi-woodland varieties where sunlight is poor can be very effective if done well.

Flat Sites

Flat sites are more common than slopes and allow alpines to be grown in most gardens. If you have a sandy soil the bed should be raised by at least 22 cm (9 in) above the surrounding ground level. If you have heavier soils raise the bed higher still. In both cases, follow the principles for construction given earlier. The soil mixture can be made to suit whatever type of growing conditions the plants you want will need.

The possibilities of a raised bed are so varied and attractive as to fire the imagination beyond the squares of grass and narrow borders so often seen and all the work is above the mud and mire of winter.

The combination of a sink garden and a pavement surrounding the raised beds, (see later chapters) opens up a new world with plenty to do but not necessarily in long stints. Twenty minutes a day in summertime is all that is needed to maintain such a combination of sites covering a total area of 200 sq metres (650 sq ft). Construction will of course take a lot longer, but if you do it in simple stages, spread over, say five years, it will give a return on the investment of your time equal to few other forms of gardening.

Chapter six

Scree Gardens

In nature a scree is created by material continuously breaking away from a mountain under the weathering action of frost and depositing itself on a slope which is also on the move downwards. The process results in the build-up towards the base of the slope of a mound, many metres deep, of variously-sized stones. It cannot be recreated exactly in a garden but a compromise is possible.

A garden possessing a gentle slope can be used to make a rock garden, or raised beds but if the site lies in full sun building a scree which is relatively easily maintained, is a wonderfully effective way of growing small alpines.

The site must have plenty of water in spring and summer to flow down to good drainage at the base. The whole site should slope between 1 in 10 and 1 in 20, sufficient to give a natural fall and to drain well in autumn and winter, when water is least needed. If the slope is too great, the scree will move too easily and, without a continuously crumbling back-up mountain to replace it, the top of the scree will disappear. The stone building up at the base is not moveable because of the plants growing along and across it.

A scree with a good depth of coarse and finer stone mixtures, combined with large stones to give a bold effect, can support a great many plants, and all of them should be in full sun. The possibilities include small-leaved cushion and mat plants, trailers, and fairly sparse shrubs, the whole creating an effect of peace and tranquillity and, above all, the im-

Scree plants as found in the wild at 4,500 metres in Kashmir.

pression of more space than there actually is. This can only be achieved in two other forms of gardening, the alpine lawn and the pavement. Unfortunately, there are few scree gardens around for you to see – all the more reason for making one.

The shape and size of a scree depend on the kind of garden into which you are putting it. The size is not important, but the scale is. A large scree in a small garden is not a good idea as it will look very flat but a scree up to approximately half the length of an open-plan garden, 10 metres (30 ft) long, can be impressive. However, if your garden is enclosed scale down the scree to a third of the total length of the garden. Unlike the rock garden and raised bed, one scree bed per garden is sufficient.

The best shape is to have the sides gently curved and the top and bottom ends dependent on the shape of the overall site. A wide site can have one curved and one squarer end (at the top); or if the site is long and narrow, both the top and base can be squared off. A scree can fit in ideally with a formally paved area at the top or base, or both, because plants can flow across the edges of the formal areas softening their lines.

Construction

The scree is basically very simple to construct but good preparation is even more vital than for any other form of construction in this book. Unlike rock gardens and raised beds, paving is not the most suitable side edging, especially where the top and base of the scree are paved, otherwise the site becomes harsh instead of flowing. Grass is probably the best material for the surround but the

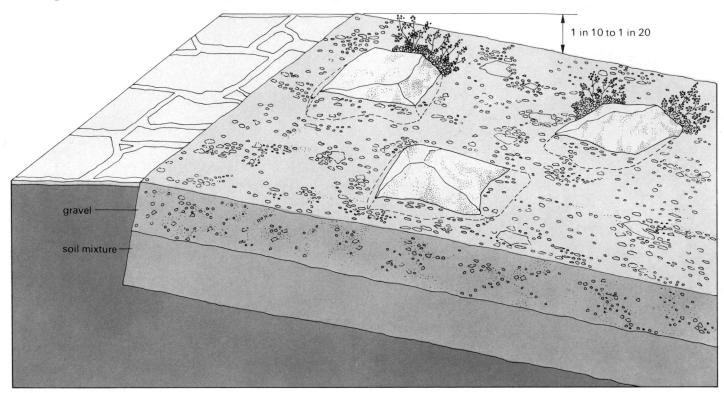

Fig. 23 Scree garden construction with slope of between 1 in 10 and 1 in 20, showing 25 cm layer of soil mixture topped with 25 cm of gravel.

1 in 10 to 1 in 20

gravel

soil mixture

warnings in previous chapters of the need for good grasses, and no creeping grasses and other weeds apply even more here, since there is no barrier to prevent invasion of the scree bed from the surrounds.

The site can be marked out simply by laying a rope or thick string round the prospective area and then cutting out the area marked to a depth of 50 cm (20 in), without using stakes first. Then remove the soil, turf or whatever covers the ground, to another part of the garden. Loosen the remaining soil with a fork before adding fresh soil in stages to prevent running over the loosened soil with the barrow.

Fill half the total depth with a soil mixture containing equal parts (by bulk) of leafmould or peat, large shingle up to 2.5 cm (1 in) in diameter and loam. If the soil is inclined to be sticky and heavy, use equal parts of leafmould or peat and shingle, with no loam. Where the soil is limy, use a limestone mixture throughout and avoid acid-loving plants. Top up all sites with gravel; from 2.5 to 5 cm (1 to 2 in) sized grains. These chippings may be acid or limestone depending on whether the plants are to be mixed limestone and acid-lovers or

just limestone plants.

The scree may be left like this but it will look more impressive and offer cooler root conditions for many plants if stone is added. Select from the types of stone used for rock gardens and raised beds and match them to the gravel or chippings. In this case, though, there is no need to match the strata and line exactly and the stones can be laid individually or in small groups, to give the impression that they have just fallen down the mountain. However you cannot just throw them in anyhow. You will have to give some thought as to how each one is arranged. Those with strata should be laid as for rock gardens, with the line of strata almost horizontal to the ground and the whole stone leaning back gently into the slope. Rounded and irregular stones can be used to give character to the otherwise flattish site; smaller stones aid good drainage.

It will be of further help to use some stones as stepping stones, to prevent too much pressure from being applied to the smaller stones around them. As they do not have to support any soil, use smaller stones than in a rock garden. Remember to avoid the 'Almond Pudding' (see

page 24) and other horrors of stones sticking up like sore thumbs! You can vary the final arrangements to suit your tastes, using from three to dozens of stones and covering up to one third of the surface area.

Maintenance
Maintenance work of course is all at ground level, so a scree is not recommended for other than reasonably agile people. However, with the large volume of stone and the shallowness of the soil, the weeding problem is greatly reduced, making this kind of garden an attractive proposition. Also, less equipment is needed to build a scree: just a spade, fork, shovel and, where grass is cut out, a halfmoon. The only large items needed are a wheelbarrow and a sack truck, which can be hired if necessary.

Watering is easily arranged. You can either use an overhead sprinkler over the whole site, or lay a hose (with a small rose attached) on the ground at the top of the scree and, with the tap on at half pressure, allow the water to flow down the site. The second system is ideal for a

Trollius europaeus, *ideal for moist sites.*

50

long narrow site on heavy soil, and can be modified to suit individual sites. Watering can be done discreetly by burying the hose permanently underground, exposing it at the end where it waters the site.

Water as and when necessary and only then. As with all rock garden sites, it is better to do the watering in the evenings as this allows the moisture to be retained instead of being taken up by the sun. A good long soaking is always preferable to an infrequent dribble of water.

The Base of the Scree
I have not mentioned the arrangements for the base of the site until now because they depend on the type of soil. Heavy soils require special arrangements and must drain to an even lower level when there is a lot of rain. Adequate drainage can be ensured by laying a single line of drainage tiles across the base of the site, on top of the soil mix, firmed down to the same level as the base of the stones laid on top of the soil.

Laying the tiles above soil level will ensure that the site never dries up completely. To allow for occasional cleaning, lay an inspection cover at the top end of the drainage system.

Planting
You may wonder how the plants are going to grow with 25 cm (10 in) of gravel or chippings between them and the soil. Plants which have grown in pots will have soil round their roots and when planted amongst the stones in the usual way and to the usual depth, will have access to the moisture held by the stones. This will support the plant roots for a short while during the growing season and encourage them to grow downwards in the search for more moisture and food. By comparison, in ordinary soils, plants tend to spread their roots in all directions, rather than just downwards. So you can see that if water is allowed to flow freely down from the top to the bottom of the scree this will further encourage growth of roots and top branches with no danger of flooding and further, that in the cold and wet seasons drainage, particularly round the necks of plants, will be perfect. In fact you will have built a modified form of what nature intended.

In planting a scree you have a great variety of alpines to choose from. As a scree is viewed from

BELOW: Pulsatilla halleri *flourishing in a scree garden.* RIGHT: *A colourful scree site supporting a variety of alpines. Note the placing of the larger stones for cooler root conditions.*

above, the bewildering effect of a variety of shapes and colours can be overcome if you plant only three or four species of particularly spiny shrubs, in a few bold groups, adding details of colour and shape from individual plants in the intervening gaps. With a bigger site you can increase the individual numbers of your favourite species.

There is no need to fill every space available. The principle of allowing spaces for further plantings later on still applies. Moreover, avoid the situation where you cannot see the stones, through overplanting.

Plant an occasional conifer in your scree, but not so many as on other sites otherwise, with their late growth and long lives, they will dominate the scene. Be careful to use trailing plants to good effect; do not allow them to swamp the cushion and mat plants. The latter are ideal for the overlapping edges between any formal paving and the scree but do not grow plants over the edges of grass, or they are bound to be chopped off during mowing and edging operations. It is better to plant the dwarf shrubs a little way in from the edge and mat plants even further in.

Although most plants tend to grow towards the sun allow them to spread in all directions equally. Plant groups of the same species within the overlapping distance given in the plants table (see pages 34 to 39) and leave enough space between to allow for more than ten years growth.

Rosette-type plants such as *Lewisia* can be planted between stones. They must be placed vertical to the ground otherwise water will rot the rosettes. This is equally true for planting in other situations but in a scree rosettes depend on closely placed stones to enable them to grow at all.

Chapter seven

Pavements

An alpine pavement is any paved area with plants growing between the slabs. This chapter deals with both using an existing paved area and building one from scratch. An existing paved area is rarely suitable as it stands, because the paving often lies on top of poor soil, rubble and rubbish left over from the building of the property which it surrounds and it therefore hides a multitude of sins. If you are planning a new pavement next to a house wall be careful not to site it above the damp course.

The first consideration when planning an alpine pavement must be drainage. This will only be a problem in areas of high flooding risk but it must always be good to a depth of 60 cm (2 ft). Follow the directions for drainage given in Chapter Two, if necessary. This will entail lifting and relaying the existing paving. If the soil is of poor quality it is best to lift all the paving and resoil the whole area to a depth of 45 cm (1½ ft). The operation will involve a lot of work but it can be done in stages, so long as you start at the lowest area to which the drainage will run, otherwise heavier soil might cause blockages and perhaps create further difficulties later on.

Shape
The pavement can be constructed in many ways. It can be built with variously-sized stone blocks laid in formal rectangular arrangements, linked like brickwork; geometric patterns can be made using squares of stone between 15 to 60 cm (6 in to 2 ft); crazy, informal paving can be

Pavement garden. Note how high the mortar comes between the paving slabs.

made by laying stones of all shapes and sizes like a jigsaw puzzle.

The idea is to plant between the paving slabs, wherever there are spaces of at least 2.5 cm (1 in). Small spaces will occur where jigsaw slabs do not match up closely and larger ones can be made by leaving out one or more slabs.

Variations
The possibilities of this type of garden can be widened by incorporating sinks into the planting areas and, where there are slopes, by making split levels with steps and walling between. The walling may be built in the same way as the sides of a raised bed and the steps can be made more formally. However the greater formality of the situation should be reflected in the design, therefore the stones must be regular in shape and laid more formally on a mortar base. If you use really large, heavy slabs on flat areas there is no need to use mortar as a bond between the soil and slabs but small stones will need it to prevent movement when the path is walked on. Both steps and walling should be firmly fitted. Make sure that the steps in particular are of a large enough size to remain stable when they are being used. If they are to be fitted without mortar, you should choose slabs which are each at least 8 kg (38 lbs) in weight. Otherwise, the slabs will have to be mortared in position in the same way as paving, see page 59. Equally, if the wall stones are to be laid in the same way as for a raised bed, see page 44, they will have to be large enough to retain the paving. If the stones are small, they will have to be mortared into position because of the pressure

from the paving stones above.

Where bricks are used for this purpose the pointing, that is the mortar between each stone, should be done in exactly the same way as for a house wall. However, if the stones being used (whether natural or artificial) are larger than house brick size, it looks much better if the pointing is rebated further in from the front, so that as little mortar as possible shows and the construction is thereby given more the appearance of a dry stone wall.

If you plan to plant in the wall or steps, leave the mortar out of any planting position, and plant when you build, as for a raised bed.

If you are building a dry stone wall it is better to lay the paving flush with the top line of stone of wall. This will prevent the danger that the overhanging slabs will dry out the wall and it will enable planting in the wall to be carried out. The mortared stones or bricks can have an overhang of paving where planting in the wall is not envisaged.

It is debatable whether there is any need to use mortar between the slabs as well as below them. Mortar certainly keeps weeds down but if, later, you have to make any changes and have not allowed for them they will be difficult to implement without disturbing other slabs. If you do lay mortar between the slabs, avoid the common mistake of making it level with the surface of the stone. It looks much more impressive when the mortar stops at least 1 cm (½ inch) from the top of the slabs, otherwise you might just as well cover the whole area with concrete and draw the lines on top; what a ghastly thought!

An attractive variation for a larger site is to surround the paved areas with raised beds as well as sinks. This gives extra scope and offers a variety of conditions (see Chapters Five and Nine) to a very wide range of plants. Take care that none of the plants gets too big, even on the largest site. Nor should any of the individual groupings be too big, so that you can reach all parts of the pavement in order to maintain it.

Maintenance

Once constructed a pavement will give the greatest pleasure with the minimum of drudgery. The areas to be maintained by weeding, watering and pruning are small in relation to the site as a whole and will always be

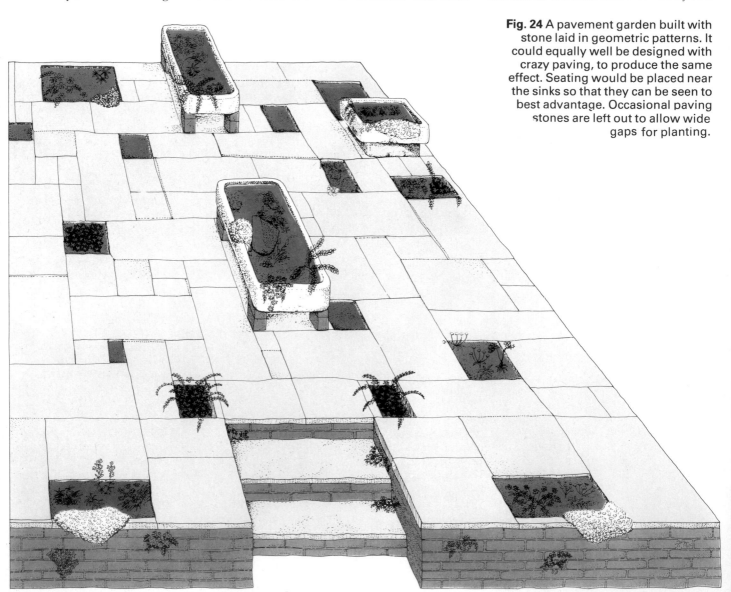

Fig. 24 A pavement garden built with stone laid in geometric patterns. It could equally well be designed with crazy paving, to produce the same effect. Seating would be placed near the sinks so that they can be seen to best advantage. Occasional paving stones are left out to allow wide gaps for planting.

easy to get at. As I advised in the chapter on rock gardens, do not contemplate highly ambitious plans unless maintenance is no problem. As a rough guide, one person should be able to look after an area of 200 sq m (217 sq yd) comfortably, working weekends and occasional evenings.

If you have a flat area of which some portion is shaded all year round, a good division of the site would be 30% for raised beds, 60% for the paved area and seating, 10% for sinks. The costs and labour can be spread over a five year period, with the construction done mainly during the winter and maintenance during the summer. Of course not all areas are going to be that straightforward; but in general best achievements can be made by tackling a small area at a time and learning as the years go by.

Stones

The paving stones do not need to be of the same variety as those used in raised beds on the site but some similarity will enhance the appearance. Composition paving may also be used. All natural stones, except the really dark ones like York paving and slates, darken with age, so bear this in mind when ordering. Ask how the stone will look in a couple of years or try to see some yourself.

Construction

Before you begin building the sink gardens or laying the paving stones, draw an overall site plan, marking

In late summer Sedum cauticolum *produces these striking flowers.*

approximate positions for the raised beds, sitting areas and sinks, then design the paving pattern. Figure 24 shows a possible arrangement. Plan to have the sinks near to windows or the seating areas, where they can be easily seen and enjoyed. Leave a large area for seating to begin with and fill it in later with plants if necessary. It is difficult to do this the other way round, especially if it involves moving some treasured plants.

Decide on which plants you would like – or at least the types (details on pages 34 to 39) – and note their flowering times before plotting their future positions, so that you can have

a balance of flowers over the site during several months of the year. You could also plan to have pockets of soil at the bottom of the raised beds; planting in these can add continuity between paving and beds.

If building raised beds and adding sinks to the site, begin by building at least one raised bed, then add the paving surrounds. Sinks can be added any time after the first section of paving has been laid but decide on their permanent position before you fill them with soil, stones and plants, after which they are very heavy. Details for constructing a sink garden are given in Chapter Nine.

Soil

As mentioned in the previous chapter, the type of soil suited to a site depends to a large extent on the amount of sunlight it receives. On a sunny site, or where the soil is heavy, use a gritty mixture, increasing the leafmould or peat content if you have a shadier garden or light soil. Gritty soil will make for better drainage, while the leafmould or peat mix will allow greater water retention. Plants in sunny situations usually require sharper drainage; those in shade need more spongy, woodland conditions. If the site is a mixture of sun and shade, try a mixture of the two soil types.

If the soil is quite good quality, that is well-drained and light, it can be incorporated into the total soil mixture. Where the paved area is bordered by clay and there is any fall in the ground, water will tend to drain from that clay producing a boggy area and artificial drainage would be essential.

Tread the soil in well to make a firm base and allow it to settle. Watering it afterwards will help – if it rains, so much the better. Soft pockets underneath will allow the slabs too much movement.

Laying the Paving Stones

When the soil has been laid to a maximum depth of 45 cm (1½ ft), pattern out the site, by laying the slabs in position on the site and then setting them aside in order. Remember to allow spaces for planting between

Planting between wall and paving with lavender to break up formal lines.

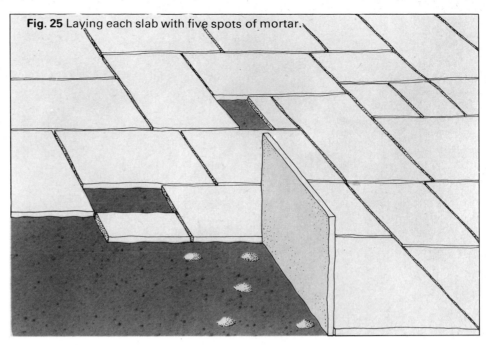

Fig. 25 Laying each slab with five spots of mortar.

the slabs. Make up the mortar from 5 parts (by bulk) builders' sand to 1 part cement, mixing it with water to the texture of toothpaste. Drop five spots, at least 5 cm (2 in) deep and 7 to 10 cm (3 to 4 in) wide on the soil, to correspond to the four outer corners and the centre of each of the stones to be laid. Small stones only need one spot. Lay each stone flat on top of the spots and tap it down with a wooden block until the stone is level and even, using a spirit level for greater accuracy see figure 25.

By laying the first paving stone in the middle of the site and moving out in all directions from it, you will be able to maintain a level, regardless of the regularity or otherwise of the individual slabs.

The distance left between each slab will depend on whether or not you have used mortar between them. If you have, allow at least 1.5 cm (½ in) between each stone, otherwise they can be laid closer together, except where you are going to add plants.

Planting

As always, choose plants to suit the soil and the climate. You will have to plant the cushion plants and bulbs in narrow spaces during construction, otherwise you will not be able to get them in at all but all other plantings can be made after the paving is completed. Remember that cushion plants should be planted with the

roots entirely underground, so it is advisable to put them in narrow gaps between the shallower slabs, which allows the tops of the plants to be above the slabs, with the roots in soil underneath.

If you have a sunny and well-drained site, you can choose from those plants coded as 'CR' in the rock garden tables on pages 34 to 39. The water-holding capacity of a pavement with vertical crevices is far greater than that of a rock garden and it will rarely need watering.

The conditions immediately under the slabs are ideal for both downward and lateral root growth and, with the top growths resting on well-drained surfaces, the plants will grow compactly provided there is no competition from others. Choose plants that are naturally matched by consulting the tables. Some plants can be walked over but you will be able to plant a greater variety of plants if this is not a consideration.

If there are larger spaces on your site you can grow deciduous shrubs and bulbous plants. The bulbs will flower when the shrubs are dormant and receive shade when the shrubs are in flower.

You can substitute trailing and mat plants for the shrubs. When the bulbs die down, the other plants come into their own.

As a general rule do not mix herbaceous plants with shrubs in a pavement, as they will swamp the shrubs.

Chapter eight

Alpine Lawns

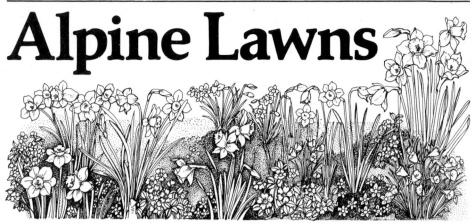

Another simple and very satisfying way of growing alpine plants is to create an alpine lawn. Its seasonal bright colours and constantly changing tints of green set off other parts of the garden in a unique way.

An alpine lawn is any stretch of grass in which alpines are grown. It does not have to be particularly flat, any angle will suffice. The quality of grass is also unimportant. In fact, it is an advantage if the grasses are not too fine, because the lawn will not be mown at all for a period of about eight months.

Because most of the plants in a lawn will be bulbs, mowing the grass has to be limited to the period when the bulbs are not actively growing, which in most cases is from June or July until October. So there will only be four or five months work on the lawn each year.

The first mowing of the year will be hard and probably require a machine. If you are not already equipped to deal with lawns, it is easiest to hire a suitable model – probably one of the large rotary mowers – once a year. Meadow grass will have reached a height of about 50 cm (20 in) when fully grown, so set the machine to its highest cutting position. The work will be easy enough if the mower has power drive on the wheels. You will have to remove the first mowings before going over the lawn on a lower cut; rake them up and compost them like ordinary mowings.

The second and subsequent cuts will be routine and an ordinary mowing machine will be adequate. Small

areas can be cut with a bill hook, if you have one, before mowing with a conventional machine but you will need to cut round any shrubs or trees in the grass with a pair of shears. Alternatively, if the lawn is very small, you can use shears to cut the whole site.

The grass will look rather yellow for two or three weeks but after that will green up well and all subsequent mowings will produce a good sward. It must be pointed out that spiking and other machinery treatments should not be used where bulbs are planted because of the damage they could cause.

Weeding

If by August your lawn is plagued with broad-leaved weeds and the growth of grasses is sufficiently strong to take the place of the weeds killed, apply a hormonal weedkiller. However, do not use weedkiller on dry ground or you will kill the grasses and bulbs as well. The brands containing 2–4-D are best and if you follow the manufacturers' instructions exactly no harm will be done to the lawn or its contents.

I mention these details at the beginning of the chapter simply because this is the hardest part of the work: the rest is so straightforward that it is surprising so few people have used this method of growing bulbs and other storage organ plants, which die down in the summer months. Crocuses and daffodils have been grown in lawns for a long time in large gardens but rarely in smaller ones. As there is now a good variety of dwarf bulbs on the market, even gardens less than 10 metres (30 ft) long can be transformed in this way.

A large alpine meadow in early April with Narcissus bulbocodium *in flower.*

Bulbs

An established lawn is perfectly suitable for conversion unless there are underlying stones or rubble to prevent planting. The quality of the lawn is bound to suffer because you cannot cut the grass so often as a top quality lawn requires but I think this is a small price to pay for the variety of colour you will see for 4–5 months of each year.

It is important to arrange the bulbs correctly: plant the larger ones furthest away and the smallest towards the front of the lawn, so that they are clearly visible. Keep the varieties of bulbs in proportion and do not mix them too much but by all means overlap them to create a natural appearance.

Bulbs can be graded according to the amount of moisture they require and also divided into sun- and shade-lovers. If there are trees on the lawn they will provide all the shade needed and this is one of the few situations where dwarf plants will not be adversely affected by the presence of trees and shrubs. Fallen leaves can be raked up to make mowing easier and do not affect the bulbs.

I have chosen the bulbs listed in the tables on pages 34 to 39 to give a spread of flowering times, yet still allow time for the grass to be cut. I have omitted some varieties because they are only suitable for larger gardens where they will grow wild if the grass is never cut. This group includes the larger *Narcissi* and *Allium*, *Eremurus*, *Camassia*, *Fritillaria imperialis* and *Zephyranthes*, some of which are tall and flower and are in leaf well into the summer.

Planting

If you are planting more than 10 bulbs, the easiest way is to scatter them gently over the ground and plant them where they land. If you have fewer than 10 bulbs, place them in groups approximately three times as far apart as the width of each bulb.

Most bulbs should be buried to a depth about double their length. Take out a plug of turf and soil as shown in figure 26 (a). When planting small bulbs and corms use a trowel; push it into the grass vertically and rock it backwards and forwards. Drop a soil mix made of three parts grit to two parts leafmould or peat into the trench formed and push the bulb into the mixture. If you are planting larger bulbs, use a spade. Cut a line vertically as with a trowel but place more than one bulb in the trenches thus formed. Make the cuts at varying angles to disguise the straight lines.

Cyclamen require different treatment. *Cyclamen cilicium*, *C. coum* and *C. hederifolium*, should be just covered by soil and *Cyclamen repandum* needs to be 7.5 cm (3 in) deep.

It is easier to plant larger grassed

LEFT: Schizostylis coccinea *in late autumn.* BELOW: Crocus aureus *in spring.*

Fig. 26 (a) For a single bulb, remove a plug of turf, add a soil mix, place in the bulb, then gently replace the plug.

For several bulbs (b) it is easier to lift a 30 cm square of turf either by dividing the square in half and folding back the turf (c) or by removing the whole square. With either method, replace the grass and gently firm in place.

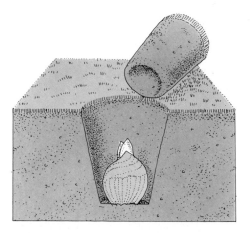

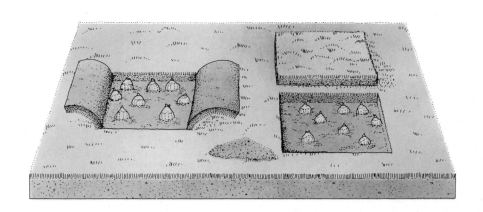

63

areas by lifting the turf in 30 cm (1 ft) squares and planting the bulbs in shallow holes, then replacing the grass see figure 26 (b) and (c). The final depth for each bulb is again about twice its height. Tread the grass down where you have made cuts and it will knit together by spring, leaving no trace. Whichever method is used, you must be careful not to leave spaces underneath the bulbs otherwise they will be left suspended in mid-air.

Planting under most trees is excellent for woodland bulbs but some trees such as birch and elm and shrubs such as privet and lilac which are surface-rooting and hungry feeders, are not suitable. In addition they all produce a mass of roots which makes it difficult to plant the bulbs in the first place. Also avoid conifers. Strangely enough, rhododendrons and magnolias, which are also surface-rooters, appear to have little or no effect on the growth of bulbs, provided that the plantings can be made between the roots and not through them.

In addition to alpine bulbs, the list

Three woodland plants for shady sites. LEFT: *Erythronium dens-canis (pink) and* Chionodoxa luciliae *(blue) flowering in late March* AND RIGHT: *the earlier-flowering Galanthus species.*

on pages 34 to 39 includes a few shrubs which are suitable for an alpine lawn; all are relatively small, keeping them in proportion with the alpines. If after some years shrubs become too large for the rock garden they can often be transplanted to the lawn, adding stature and height to an otherwise level surface.

Chapter nine

Sink Gardens

For the beginner there can be no form of gardening more exciting and rewarding than growing a wide variety of plants in containers raised to any chosen level. Several sink gardens take up very little space and each can have a different soil mixture and therefore support a whole range of plants. Moreover, the gardens will last many years. They are particularly suitable for disabled people in wheelchairs or those who are not very mobile, as they do not need to involve bending.

The original sink gardens were made in sinks carved from solid blocks of stone but these have become scarce and very expensive. With a little ingenuity, people turned to the glazed sinks which replaced the stone ones. No doubt in years to come the pressed steel units which are replacing glazed sinks will themselves be put into service.

It is still possible to get hold of glazed sinks but unfortunately many are smashed up. Do try to get hold of one if you possibly can; they are usually free and many are dumped on commons and other open spaces. Your local plumber might know of a source.

Other materials can be used to contain a sink garden and the larger the container, the wider the variety of alpines you can grow.

Moulded concrete makes excellent sink gardens of any (reasonable) size, although this will be limited if you need to cast in one place and erect in another. Sinks made of bricks or stone laid on a concrete base also can be built to any reasonable size, i.e.

A real stone sink with a full complement of planting, perfectly balanced.

any size which can be planted, maintained and observed easily. In fact the possibilities are endless but I would not recommend using plastic or other synthetic materials because they look garish and artificial. This may sound surprising when I have already suggested using concrete but this material can at least be made to look like old stone, whereas plastics can never look other than what they are, with their unnatural colours.

As with any method of growing alpines, preparation is all important and takes time.

Glazed Sinks

Glazed sinks are made in various sizes and depths. The deeper ones are preferable, offering space for a greater range of plants.

To improve the appearance of the sink you will need a cement weld, cement, sand and peat. Clean the sink thoroughly, and remove any piping still attached to the drainage hole. Mount the sink on a block so that you can reach underneath. Note that it is much easier to carry out the following stage in the cool, frost free autumn months. Paint a cement weld over one end, over the lip and 8 cm (3 in) down the inside and about 10 cm (4 in) underneath. When the adhesive is tacky, apply a prepared mixture made from 1 part (by bulk) cement, 1 part sand and 1 or 2 parts thoroughly moistened moss peat. Pass the peat through a 1.5 cm (½ in) sieve before measuring it. Add water to the mix and stir until it is stiff enough to hold without dry crumbling but not so soft that it oozes out. Then, wearing household rubber gloves, apply the mix in small handfuls to the surface of the adhesive. It may tend to slip off but persevere until you find the knack of making it stick. Spread a layer about 1.5 cm (½ in) thick all over, rounding off the inside edges and underneath where it finishes. The proportion of peat you use will affect the texture; the more peat, the darker and rougher it will be. Repeat with the other sides.

To start with make enough of the mixture to fill a standard-sized galvanized bucket and mix a further amount as you need it. The first time you will need to allow at least two hours for the whole job but with practice it will become easier and much quicker.

You can create a stippled finish over the surface by poking it with your fingers and if you leave it unpolished the finish will look even more natural. The following day paint the treated area with a seaweed feed, manure water, or milk to encourage the growth of green algae, which will 'age' the surface and make it look more like natural stone.

If the sink is standing outside cover it with a plastic sheet to protect it from rain for two days; if it is already under cover take it outside to weather after the two days. Allow the mix to cure for three weeks before planting. Handle the sink with great care when it is being moved because the mix can easily be chipped. Once in position the surface is hardwearing unless badly knocked.

Sinks from Railway Sleepers
Lengths of railway sleepers can be joined together with aluminium angle brackets (you could use steel but they will rust), see figure 27. The brackets can be painted brown or black to match the sleepers, and make a sturdy and manageable container. The drainage holes should be drilled at 30 cm (1 ft) intervals and each one 2.5 cm (1 inch) wide.

Concrete Sinks
Making a concrete sink is a more involved process requiring a wooden mould and reinforcements to strengthen the finished product. You will only make one size of sink per mould but in compensation alpines can be planted literally all over a concrete sink, because holes can be drilled into its sides. (The sides of sinks made of stones or railway

Fig 27

sleepers are too thick to be planted.)

To make a wooden mould for the concrete use 12 mm (½ in) thick deal for all parts unless otherwise stated and first make a flat, rectangular base slightly larger than the size of container you want, then make two sides and two ends to fit exactly inside and on to the base, to the required height (at least 20 cm (8 in) and not more than 30 cm (1 ft)). Make sure that the sides are shorter by the thickness of the wood at each end, so that the sides fit within the ends, as shown in figure 28.

To make the inside mould, cut the same shaped sides and ends again, but smaller, to allow a gap between the moulds at the sides and ends of 3 cm (1¼ in) and 5 cm (2 in) between the bases. The base of the inner mould is best in thin wood, cut to fit within the inner mould, not below it. Cut 8 lengths of deal 2.5 cm × 2.5 cm × 5 cm (1 × 1 × 2 in) for the inner mould, one for each corner, and nail to the sides and ends on the inside of the mould to form a box, leaving the heads of the nails protruding for easy removal later on.

Then cut 8 lengths of 5 cm × 2.5 cm (2 × 1 in) deal, 6 20 cm (4 in) longer than the sides of the outer mould and 2 20 cm (4 in) longer than the ends. Next cut 16 blocks 5 × 2.5 × 10 cm (2 × 1 × 4 in). Nail one block to each end of the 8 lengths and

arrange the pieces as shown in figure 28. Do not nail any of the outer mould parts together. Make up the concrete mix. It is one part (by bulk) cement, two parts coarse sand or fine grit and one part sieved peat, with sufficient water to produce a toothpaste-like texture, soft enough to poke into narrow spaces. Do not make it too wet or the air spaces created when it dries out will weaken the whole structure.

Fill the base of the mould with a 5 cm (2 in) layer of concrete mix, then fit the inner mould on top. First position the base and then the sides, now nailed together. Weight the base with bricks.

If you want planting holes in the concrete, drill holes 2.5 cm (1 in) in diameter in the sides and ends of the outer mould and slightly larger ones in the inner mould, making sure that they line up. If you fit bungs tapered from the inside outwards, you can plant in the resulting holes in the finished container. Holes tapering in the opposite direction will gradually fill up with debris and eventually block the hole. You must cut one hole 5 cm (2 in) wide in the middle of the base for drainage and use a large bung to fit.

Fill the spaces between the mould with concrete, tamping well down as you do so, leaving the top rough.

To give the concrete added

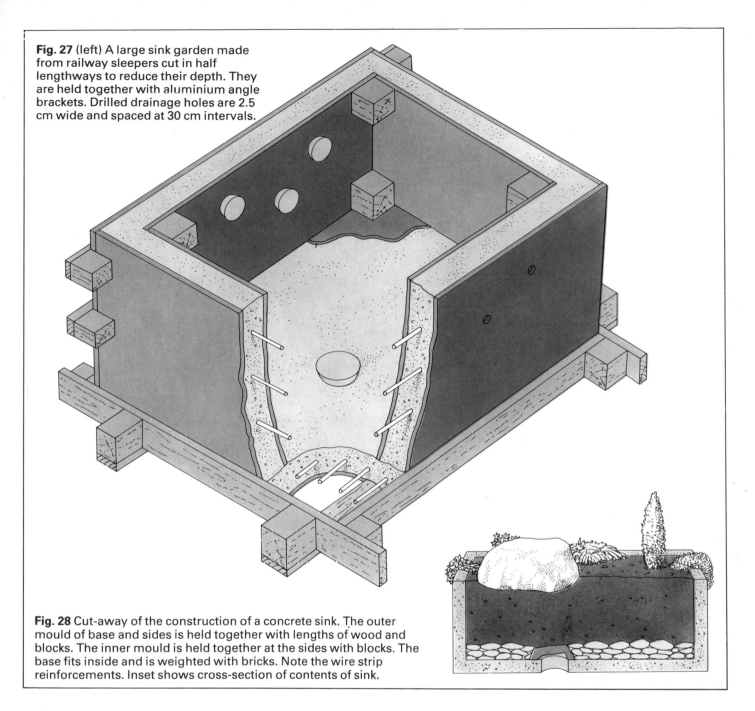

Fig. 27 (left) A large sink garden made from railway sleepers cut in half lengthways to reduce their depth. They are held together with aluminium angle brackets. Drilled drainage holes are 2.5 cm wide and spaced at 30 cm intervals.

Fig. 28 Cut-away of the construction of a concrete sink. The outer mould of base and sides is held together with lengths of wood and blocks. The inner mould is held together at the sides with blocks. The base fits inside and is weighted with bricks. Note the wire strip reinforcements. Inset shows cross-section of contents of sink.

strength, especially at the corners, reinforce it with 2 mm ($\frac{1}{12}$ in) gauge wire. As long as none of the wire touches the moulds, oxygen will be excluded and the wire will not rust. Fit it in 20 cm (8 in) lengths, particularly around the corners, from the sides to ends and from the sides and ends to the base.

After four days remove the bungs by first gently tapping them from the outside, then remove the outside lengths of wood from the top and sides then the corner blocks from the inner mould by removing the nails. Gently tap down on all the wood of

both moulds and remove them. You will have to leave the inner base where it is because it will be well wedged in.

Turn the newly-made container on its side to remove the last outer lengths of wood at the base. Tap out the base bung and finally, remove the outer base.

With a pointed cold chisel and club hammer, roughen the outside of the container and, when it looks less like a concrete box, paint the sides, ends and top edges with seaweed feed, manure water or milk to age its appearance.

Mount the sink on two lengths of wood and leave it to cure, under cover, for five weeks. If you are doing this in the autumn, the curing time will take longer making the sink stronger as a result.

Brick Sinks
It is far simpler to make a sink from bricks set on a concrete base than an all-concrete one. Carry out the construction on sheets of newspaper larger than the container.

Cut four lengths of wood 5 × 2.5 cm (2 × 1 in) – two of the proposed length of the container and

Fig. 29 A framework of lengths of wood held together with blocks make a mould for a concrete base. A tapered round of wood makes the drainage hole.

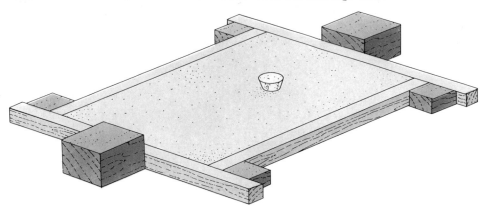

Fig. 30 Cut-away of the construction of a brick sink, showing spaces left in mortar for planting. The drainage is central so the supports will be at the corners.

two of 15 cm (6 in) longer. The wood should be clean and deal is cheapest. Nail blocks of deal 5 × 5 × 2.5 cm (2 × 2 × 1 in) to the ends of the longer pieces. Fit the long pieces within the blocks of end pieces to form a rectangle and put heavy blocks against the ends to hold them in place when the concrete is poured into the frame. Use the same concrete mix as for a concrete sink but reinforce it with strips of metal sandwiched in the concrete in the shape of a series of crosses. The amount of reinforcement needed depends on the size of the base. Small sinks up to 40 cm by 30 cm (15 in by 12 in) with a depth of 25 cm (10 in) do not need reinforcement but it is necessary for sinks larger than these dimensions.

Fit tapered rounds of wood to make drainage holes – roughly one drainage hole, 5 cm (2 in) in diameter, for every square metre (sq yd) of base. Make the base about 5 cm (2 in) thick with the bungs spaced out over the base and leave for four days before removing the frame and bungs, then chip and paint the sides and ends as suggested before. Remember the base will have to be mounted, so the placing of the bungs will depend on the type of mounting.

The base can now be placed in its permanent position, and the bricks or stone built on to it. Mortar them together with a mixture of 3 parts (by bulk) sand to 1 part cement and build up the sides to the required height, never more than 40 cm (16 in). Try to use old bricks to give the sink a weathered look.

Leave spaces between some of the end joints of bricks, or at any points between the stones, for vertical planting. Allow the construction to cure for three weeks, then plant.

Positioning the Sink
All sinks and containers must be raised above ground to allow for drainage. The height at which they stand depends on what and whom they are for. The ideal height of a sink for a disabled person in a wheelchair or someone who is happier working sitting down rather than standing is 60–75 cm (2–2½ ft) to the top of the sink. Those who operate best standing, must raise the sink to suit their own needs, but do not mount it too high or it will become unstable. For the able bodied a height of 15 cm (6 in) from the ground to the base of the sink is perfect and the sink can easily be made stable by placing one or more stones or a few old bricks beneath it.

The choice of mountings for the containers will depend on the overall size and the position of the drainage holes. Any sinks above the dimensions of 60 cm by 30 cm (24 in by 12 in) should ideally have supports around the edges and a central drainage hole, whilst those at or below these measurements can be centrally supported with drainage at one end.

Put sinks of any size in their permanent positions before adding soil, stone or plants because they become extremely heavy and difficult to move once filled.

Positioning sinks is important. They should be as near to the house as possible and sinks for the disabled and elderly should be on firm foundations, next to a path without any kind of obstruction. A good position is on a paved area, particularly close to a sitting-out area which is ideal for viewing and bringing the garden almost into the home. Where there is no paving, plant the area immediately around and below the container to soften and broaden its effect, leaving enough room for maintenance of the sink.

A balcony is a good place for a sink garden. There are many advantages,

especially if it can be built on the site. The exposed setting is ideal for cushion, rosette and mat plants and even a windy site will not harm these plants – quite the reverse, in fact.

Filling the Sink
Cover the drainage hole(s) with a piece of perforated zinc, fine-mesh nylon netting, screwed-up chicken wire or any other material which will allow water but not soil out through the drainage hole. If you use nylon netting it must stretch across a large enough area for the soil to hold it taut so that it does not fall through the drainage hole. At the bottom of the sink put a 4 cm (1½ in) layer of thoroughly moistened coarse peat or upturned and well-rotted turves or, if the sink is a deep one, broken clay pots or bricks, or coarse gravel to act as drainage filters. There is no point in using these crocks for a shallow sink where all the space is needed for the roots to grow and, a shallow container is more easily drained.

Add the soil mix, ramming each layer down hard until it reaches 5 cm (2 in) from the top. As always, the soil mix will depend on the plants being used; follow the instructions for the rock garden and raised beds, laying slightly more emphasis on drainage because in winter and heavy rains, the sink garden will not drain as freely through one hole as does the base of an open planting. During the growing season more watering will be necessary than with other sites. Use a watering can or a hosepipe with a rose in the end. If, as suggested, the sinks are near the house, this should not present any problems.

Where there are holes in the sides of the container choose plants to suit the direction they will face. Plant when the soil inside is on a level with the hole. Push the plants from the inside outwards, not the other way round, making sure that the roots are always covered. Fill any gaps left around the plants with fresh mortar.

To diminish the flat effect at the surface of the sink add one or more large stones to give height, proportion and planting spaces, just like a miniature rock garden. Use any kind

Three specially weathered concrete sinks combined with a pavement garden.

LEFT: Adiantum pedatum, *a fern for a shady place in the sink or larger site.* ABOVE RIGHT: Erodium reichardii *and* BELOW RIGHT: Asperula suberosa, *both for sunny situations in a sink or pavement or for crevice planting.*

of stone that matches the type of soil used and preferably one with some character; for instance put limestone with lime-loving plants. Westmorland is ideal for this. Tufa (see page 13) is excellent in a sink, because holes can be cut, filled with soil and then planted. A big piece can be used as a sink garden in its own right. Other stones though are also very good when used boldly and you can create steep slopes by running them into the soil at a slightly exaggerated angle. There are so many possible arrangements that I suggest you try several ways before committing the plants to their final positions. After all, the sink is, hopefully, going to last for 15 years and even though you will probably make alterations to the planting, to remove stone requires complete renewal of the sink. However, do not bury the stone unnecessarily.

Planting

Plan which plants should go where carefully. For instance, do not allow a trailing plant to grow over a cushion and avoid any conical planting right in the middle of the sink. Keep the taller plants towards a corner and limit their number.

When the plant is removed from its container, plant it so that the top 5 cm (2 in) is above the level of the soil in the sink, thus exposing the roots and topsoil, and the base of the top of the plant is on a level with the top of the container. To make a better finish fill the 5 cm (2 in) space with matching stone chippings if the garden is in a sunny situation. This not only improves the appearance but also provides perfect drainage round the necks of the plants and creates spaces for water to percolate down without muddy splashings. For the shady setting use fine forest bark instead of chippings.

Follow the codes used in the table in Chapter Four to choose suitable plants, though only experience will show which look well together and how best to grow them.

Chapter ten

Care Calendar

You cannot build a rock garden or allied sites and then conveniently leave them to maintain themselves. Therefore, this chapter will guide you in dividing the time to enable the various aspects of construction and maintenance to be carried out. The least amount of routine garden maintenance will need to be done in winter, when it is cold, so that is the best time to begin the construction of any site and to carry out the heaviest work.

The busiest time is spring, when construction is being completed and planting, mowing and the routine garden tasks are carried out, reaching a height of activity around Easter. So plan and prepare shortly after the spring for the following autumn.

Alpine nurseries can be visited at any time of year but you will probably have more free time in the summer.

January

Construction work on all sites can begin this month, weather permitting. Avoid heavy work immediately after hard frosts, or after rain or snow when the ground is very soft; it is much better to wait until it dries out.

In frosty weather large stones can be easily moved over hard ground and placed near the site, even though they cannot be laid.

After frosts check that glass covers over the plants have not been dislodged from the wires, and that the wires are still securely in the ground.

Anemone blanda *with* Draba aizoides *(yellow) in early spring. The anemone dies down in May.*

Make sure that the labels are still firmly fixed and legible.

Remove any dead leaves from all sites and cut dead branches from shrubs with sharp secateurs.

Most alpine seeds are sent out from mid-winter onwards and should be sown as soon as possible after they arrive.

Take cuttings from the fleshy rooted plants as described on page 19. Plants which can be propagated this way are: *Anchusas, Armerias, Codonopsis, Convolvulus, Dicentras, Erodiums, Eryngiums, Euphoribias, Geraniums, Lewisias, Morisias, Papavers, Platycodons* and *Verbascums.*

February

Construction can continue at a greater pace this month.

On warmer days start weeding–a little and often rather than occasional long stretches. Try to weed before the plants go to seed, especially between bulbs. As long as the weather is not too wet or frosty, apply pre-emergence weedkillers from this month onwards. Use simazine combined with paraquat for annual weeds. Follow the manufacturer's instructions exactly and apply using a bottle sprayer *with a guard on.* Do not use weedkillers when it is windy and only spray paths and paved areas where you are certain there are no wanted plants. Check labels and glass covers again, as in January.

Continue pruning dead wood from shrubs and sowing seeds. Some seeds will start to germinate this month. Prick them out into seed trays and pot up seedlings. Labelled crevice plants can be sown.

75

March

Construction should be reaching a climax now and spring planting started if the weather is suitable. Always label as you plant.

Continue weeding and, using a handfork, break up the soil gently round the plants, firming any plants which have been lifted by the frost. Where glass is covering plants check that it is still necessary, i.e. when the weather is cold and damp most of the time. Remove it from plants in growth and store it, cleaned, until next winter.

Cut back all old herbaceous material which died down the previous autumn to ground level; prune Fuchsias to within 5 cm (2 in) of soil. Feed the soil in shady areas with a mulch of fine forest bark, leafmould, hops or well-rotted garden compost. In exposed areas spread it about 3 cm (1 in) thick every third year. All areas will benefit from an annual feed of bonemeal at the rate of 35 g per square metre (1 oz per sq yd), which can be applied this month. Top dress any sunken parts of the garden with the same mixture used when they were first planted.

Make a plan of plants in each area, plotting them precisely where possible and noting all those that die down to nothing during winter (plants hidden underground as bulbs and other storage organs).

Keep grass edges round lawns trimmed.

Pricking out and potting up should be in full swing as seedlings germinate and grow rapidly.

Complete propagation by division since growth is starting now. Divide herbaceous plants and those with multiple stems, from ground level.

April

A very busy month. Construction and spring planting should be completed this month now that growth is in earnest. Some plants such as *Codonopsis* will still be dormant. Continue to weed and hand fork the ground each month. Complete the feeding, mulching and top dressing of the soil.

Remove all remaining glass covers. It may be necessary to shade glass or plastic propagation frames in warmer parts of the country, if the weather is warm and sunny during at least part

of the day.

Seedlings and root cuttings which show top growth, should be pricked out and potted up. Continue to do this throughout the spring and summer.

Layering of plants for replacement should be done this month. If you pot a few more seedlings than you need yourself, they can be exchanged with friends or given away.

Trim lawn edges each week from now until September-October, and fork out any creeping grasses and weeds that appear around the sites.

May

The propagation frames will need more shading. Covers should be used on all bright days and removed on dull days and when natural shading is cast.

It may be necessary to start watering areas other than sinks, if the top 8 cm (3 in) of soil dries out. Water thoroughly, then leave for as long as possible.

Start collecting ripened seed of alpines and store in dry envelopes or cartons in the shade.

In late May plant out annual alpines not listed in this book and seedlings potted up earlier in the year. Label carefully. (The plants in this book have been selected from the vast numbers available especially because they are long-lived.)

Spray against aphids (green, black or grey fly) as soon as they are seen and continue throughout the summer, repeating the procedure every ten days, using one of the various proprietary products available. Aphids carry dangerous virus diseases, so their immediate reduction is vital.

June

As the large trailing plants, such as *Aubrieta*, *Helianthemum*, finish flowering, cut them hard back removing previous year's growth, to encourage plenty of flowers next year. Also cut back those plants which are stronger than they appeared earlier in the year, to prevent them invading other plants, by removing individual branches. Remember: pruning makes for strong growth.

Regular watering may be necessary by now. Try to do it in the evenings when the weather is cooler, so that the water lasts longer around the plants.

There is more seed to collect now. Take nodal and heel cuttings off many alpines this month, (see Chapter Three, page 18), as growth is firming up but not yet hard.

July

Continue watering unless storms make it unnecessary.

Seed collecting is now at its height and should continue until September. Clean seeds in preparation for sowing.

Take more cuttings as in June.

Prune trailing plants after flowering to keep growth bushy.

By now bulbs will have died down and alpine lawns can have their first mowing and trimming.

Have a look at alpine nurseries and gardens during the summer holiday months.

ABOVE LEFT: Campanula carpatica *and* BELOW LEFT: Dianthus *'Little Jock' both seen in mid-summer.* BELOW: Daphne collina *(pink) and* Cytisus kewensis.

August

Continue to trim back and prune after trailing plants have flowered. Watering may not be needed.
Plant alpine bulbs.
Take heel cuttings from the more woody alpines, but not conifers.
Weekly mowing of alpine lawns can now be merged with other mowing.

September

Begin to construct and plant rock gardens, raised beds, pavements, sink gardens and screes.
Shades on propagating frames are only needed during the warmest part of the day when the sun is out.
Take conifer and *Aubrieta* cuttings.
Water only when necessary.
Plant alpine bulbs.
Update the plan in case labels disappear during winter.

October

Construction, with crevice planting only, on any site. Good month for making reproduction sinks i.e. any container other than a true stone sink. Label and list all crevice plants.
Take shading off propagating frames until next April.
Put glass covers on all cushion plants marked in the tables.
Order seed lists (if not already done).
Take conifer and *Aubrieta* cuttings.
Remove fallen leaves weekly now.

November

Construction can take place on all sites; another good month for sinks.
Crevice planting only. List all plants on the plan after labelling. Check that glass covers are firm.
Remove leaves off all alpine areas as they fall, leaving the stems and leaves of herbaceous plants exposed until next year.
Divide herbaceous plants.

December

Construction can take place with crevice planting on all sites. This is also a good month for reproduction sinks. Label and list as planting is carried out. Check that glass covers are firm.
Remove leaves and fallen branches.

LEFT: Cyclamen coum *in early January.*
ABOVE RIGHT: Sanguinaria canadensis plena *in late spring.* BELOW RIGHT: Soldanella alpina *growing wild.*

Index

ACKNOWLEDGEMENTS

The publishers would like to thank the following individuals and organizations for their kind permission to reproduce the pictures in this book:
A–Z Botanical Collection 26, 53, 62; Heather Angel/Biofotos 18, 48–49, 51, 78; Ardea (Bob Gibbons) 1, 79 below right, (Sue Gooders) 47, (J. L. Mason) 57; Pat Brindley 4–5, 10 above left, 11, 15, 22, 25, 46, 65, 71, 76 above and below right; Bruce Coleman Ltd. (Hans Reinhard) 8–9, (Eric Crichton) 30–31, (John Sims) 58, (N. Fox-Davies) 63; Valerie Finnis 20–21, 28, 64, 74–75, 77; Leslie Johns and Associates 16–17, 52, 60–61; Palma Studio 6; The Harry Smith Horticultural Photographic Collection 2–3, 10 below left, 40–41, 44–45, 54–55, 66, 72, 73 above and below right, 79 above right; Michael Warren 12–13, 42
Cover Photograph: **Pamla Toler**
All step by step illustrations drawn by **Allard Studios**.
Chapter illustrations drawn by **Vana Haggerty**.